Praise for *Let's Retire Retirement*

"*Let's Retire Retirement* captures what so many of us have felt but struggled to articulate: The idea of 'retirement' no longer serves our evolving lives. Derek Coburn issues a bold invitation to rethink your approach to time and money—and to reassess what makes life meaningful."

DANIEL H. PINK, #1 *New York Times*-bestselling author of *The Power of Regret*, *When*, and *Drive*

"A generous, actionable, and useful book—a chance to find connection and meaning by producing value, even as others retire and retreat."

SETH GODIN, author of *This Is Marketing*

"Under the pretense of a 'finance' book, *Let's Retire Retirement* is really a love letter on pursuing a life well lived written by someone who genuinely, desperately wants you to find your best path. Derek Coburn understands human instincts well enough to know that to get you there he has to show you—practically, with extensive data and compelling anecdotes—that you can, and should, YOLO your way from now right through your own final chapter. You will surely be richer after reading this 'finance' book, but maybe not in the way you think."

CHRISTIAN GENETSKI, president of FanDuel Group

"What if instead of retiring, you planned to earn an income in some capacity for the rest of your life? How different would your life be today? *Let's Retire Retirement* walks you through the opportunities that open up when you start thinking this way, and gives you practical examples of how to do it."
NATHAN BARRY, founder and CEO of Kit

"*Let's Retire Retirement* is a powerful reminder that the ultimate measure of success is building a life and career so fulfilling you'd never dream of leaving it behind. Derek Coburn is the perfect guide for anyone striving to harmonize purpose and prosperity. If you aren't ready to settle for a life that is anything less than everything you've ever wanted—at every stage and at every age—this book is essential."
LAURA GASSNER OTTING, ABC contributor and *Wall Street Journal*-bestselling author of *Wonderhell*

**LET'S RETIRE
RETIREMENT**

LET'S RETIRE RETIREMENT

HOW TO ENJOY LIFE TO THE FULLEST—NOW AND LATER

DEREK COBURN

WITH SARA STIBITZ

Copyright © 2025 by Derek Coburn

All rights reserved. No part of this book may be reproduced, stored in a retrieval system or transmitted, in any form or by any means, without the prior written consent of the publisher or a license from The Canadian Copyright Licensing Agency (Access Copyright). For a copyright license, visit accesscopyright.ca or call toll free to 1-800-893-5777.

The information and materials provided in this book are for informational purposes only and do not constitute legal, financial, or other professional advice. Readers are encouraged to seek the advice of a qualified financial advisor or legal professional before making any decisions based on the content of this book. The author and publisher disclaim any liability for any losses or damages incurred as a result of actions taken based on the information provided.

Some names and identifying details have been changed to protect the privacy of individuals.

Cataloguing in publication information is available from Library and Archives Canada.
ISBN 978-1-77458-506-1 (paperback)
ISBN 978-1-77458-507-8 (ebook)

Page Two
pagetwo.com

Cover design by Peter Cocking
Interior design and illustration by Cameron McKague
Printed and bound in Canada by Friesens
Distributed in Canada by Raincoast Books
Distributed in the US and internationally by Macmillan

25 26 27 28 29   5 4 3 2 1

derekcoburn.com

Contents

Preface *1*
Introduction *5*

PART ONE Rethinking Retirement

1. Retirement Is Not Working *19*
2. How We Got Here: The History of Retirement *35*
3. Happiness versus Meaning *49*
4. The Questions You Need to Be Asking *61*
5. Your Many Options *77*
6. The Changing World of Work *105*

PART TWO Financial Planning for Nontraditional Retirees

7. How to Set Up Your Financial Plan *119*
8. Insurance: Protection for the Future *137*
9. Investment Strategies *155*
10. Investing in You *177*

Conclusion *201*
Acknowledgments *205*
Notes *209*
Index *219*

Preface

I STARTED WRITING this book in 2017, and it took seven years to finish it. Life, family, and my work took up most of my time. Like anyone else who has attempted to write a book, my unfinished work always sat in the back of my mind. I went almost four years without changing much of the manuscript, in large part because of COVID and everything that came with it. Something else changed for me too—the way I viewed my father's life in relation to his own retirement.

In 2013, at the age of 62, my father started to act differently. He slowed down and began to make more mistakes. He was a certified public accountant (CPA), so mistakes were a clear sign that something was wrong. We soon found out that these were early signs of dementia.

In 2017, when I started writing this book, my father was pretty far gone. He still seemed to recognize me, but I was never sure. He was disoriented. He didn't recognize his grandkids or his family most of the time.

In the years before his diagnosis, my father and I had talked about his retirement. I felt sad for him as I wrote this book;

I felt that if I had written it a decade ago, he would have enjoyed his life more, would have spent more of his time and money on things he wanted to do while he was in a better state.

My father passed away in April 2022. With his death came many conversations with family and many memories of my father. I remembered being a 10-year-old boy whose father was around every single day when he got home from school. In fact, he had turned down a partnership offer with a big CPA practice in Baltimore, Maryland, so that he could be with his family. Dad made his office in the basement of our house with a desk made out of an old door placed on supports.

He did people's taxes on his own time. He never missed any of my sporting events. I played sports every season of the year, and so did my brother and sister. We took one or two family vacations every single year. After my dad passed, I realized I hadn't properly acknowledged that my father had sacrificed a lot of money and security to be there for his kids and his family.

He still did a great job saving even though he took a significant pay cut to work the way he did. He still had ideas and thoughts about what he wanted to do when he retired. He loved his work, but he also loved to spend time with my mom. As I went through old photos after he passed, I realized I hadn't appreciated how much traveling he and my mom had done after I left the house. They took trips to Italy and other European countries, cruised in Alaska, and visited my sister in California.

Before he developed dementia symptoms, my father and I had more and more conversations that were entrepreneurial in nature. He invested money in a few start-ups and asked for my feedback on various business ideas, so we began bonding in new ways. It didn't dawn on me until after he died that he might never have retired, because he had carved out a life for himself where he loved the work he was doing, felt engaged by new ideas and opportunities, and enjoyed a lot of time with his loved ones.

My father provided the blueprint not only for this book but also for my life. He left opportunity on the table to be with his family and spend time with the people he cared about. I went from thinking that my dad was buying into traditional retirement and forgoing a lot of enjoyment in his life to realizing that, for the most part, he did what he wanted to do when he wanted to do it.

I now see that in the last five years, I was living a lot of what I'm going to be sharing in this book. I've been incredibly mindful about the amount of time I spend with my family and chosen family—the term my wife and I use to describe the relationship we have with many of our close friends. There have been a lot of concerts, a lot of travel, and in the case of my nuclear family, I've carved out time almost every day to be available to them.

I want to dedicate this book to my father. Thank you for the lessons you taught me and the example you set for me. I only wish that you could have read this book and come to know the positive impact your choices had on me and so many others.

Introduction

WHEN I began to think about writing this book, I was under the impression that many of us were saving so much that we were collectively forgoing meaningful life experiences in the name of boosting our retirement accounts. As a financial advisor, it was common for me to tell a client to quit saving so much and start using some of that money to enjoy their life now.

But the more research I did, and the more I talked with people about the concept for this book, the more I realized that most people are *not* on track for retirement, and they have no idea that they don't have to retire the way everyone has told them they should. To make matters worse, most people feel some sense of anxiety around their future. Their fear around retirement leads to either overworking or avoiding the topic altogether.

These fears aren't off base either. In fact, for most Americans, the concept of traditional retirement is dead on arrival. According to a study done by the Alliance for Lifetime Income's Retirement Income Institute, most Americans who turn 65 between 2024 and 2030 have not saved enough for full retirement.[1] Over half (52.5 percent) have saved $250,000 or less, which makes it highly likely they will run out of money if they fully retire at 65.[2] There are vast differences between demographics too. While the median savings for the age group referenced above is $225,000, the numbers vary between sexes: men have saved $269,000 whereas women have saved only $185,000. The median savings rate of white Americans is $299,000, a stark contrast to the median savings rates of Hispanic Americans and Black Americans, which are $123,000 and $49,000, respectively.[3]

It's not just those close to retirement who are behind in saving. A study done by the National Institute on Retirement Security found that 66 percent of Millennials have nothing saved for retirement; they've spent most of their careers focused on paying off student debt and trying to get into the increasingly competitive housing market.[4] Gen Xers aren't much better off: 22 percent have over $500,000 saved, but 25 percent have less than $10,000.[5] The majority of the rest fall somewhere in between—and they're not far off from hitting 65.

These numbers are terrifying.

Americans are doing whatever they can to save, but they already know it's never going to be enough to support themselves. They pinch and save in the hopes they'll catch up. They're stressed to the max about saving for retirement while having to pay for school for their children. Because they feel so short on money, they sacrifice their time, their vacation days, and their health to continue working longer and longer hours. They try to alleviate that distress by choosing not to pursue the work they love—that typically pays less—because they think that they have to keep plugging away to reach their goal—after which they hope to relax and enjoy their lives.

This attitude leads to an incredible amount of stress and missed opportunities to enjoy life now. A 2023 Pew Research

Center survey shows that 46 percent of US workers failed to use all their paid time off.[6] What's more, the amount of paid time off we have isn't enough in the first place. Expedia does an annual survey and produces the aptly named *Vacation Deprivation Report*, which looks at the vacation habits of over 14,000 workers in North and South America, Europe, and the Asia-Pacific region. In 2023, workers in the US received an average of only 12.5 vacation days to use in a year, compared to 22 vacation days in Japan, and 28.5 in France and Germany.[7] Sixty-five percent of respondents reported using their vacation days for things like personal appointments, and 56 percent used them for sick days.[8] However you look at it, we're overworking ourselves to save money.

A quote often attributed to the Dalai Lama describes this paradox perfectly: What is most surprising about humans is they sacrifice their health in order to make money. Then they sacrifice money to recuperate their health. And then they are so anxious about the future that they do not enjoy the present; the result being that they do not live in the present or the future; they live as if they are never going to die, and then die having never really lived.

I believe that deep down we already know this is a losing game, but we haven't course-corrected yet—we're still putting off valuable time with our loved ones or waiting for retirement to enjoy our money or pursue our dreams. Most of us are experiencing an incredible amount of stress about our financial futures—all because of an idea that we're supposed to hit some "magic number" by the time we turn 65. Because we're so unhappy now, we choose to believe that traditional retirement puts us on the path to future happiness.

I'm going to break this to you now. Because so few of us are on track to traditionally retire, the reality is that few of us will *actually* retire at the age of 65 and live a life of leisure. This includes you. I say 65 because that is the age that comes to mind for most people when they think about retirement and is often the age used most by the financial services industry for planning purposes.

And...

This doesn't have to be bad news.

The Myth of Traditional Retirement

We've all been sold the idea of the hard-stop retirement, but it's a myth. I want you to get excited instead about what life might be like if you extend your career and find meaningful work that gives you satisfaction well into your 70s and 80s. If you're waiting for retirement to be happy, you don't have to wait that long.

Anyone who accepts or is excited about traditional retirement is already buying into the notion that their life is going to be better later than it is now. Why else would you forgo experiences and time with your friends and family now in exchange for these experiences in the future? I want you to consider that the good life is already accessible to you, maybe even closer than you think, and you don't have to sacrifice all your time or money to experience it.

Since I started writing this book, people from all walks of life have shared their stories with me. At a conference, a 78-year-old woman told me her father once said she shouldn't ever retire, that she should enjoy her time with her family and plan on working longer. She took his advice and started a new job with a legal company at the age of 75. "It's been the best three years of my life," she told me. Another friend told me he was going to sell his business when a colleague told him not to do it. His colleague's father sold his business and then suffered for the next 10 years because his new life seemed to lack meaning and purpose. My friend decided to

If you're waiting for retirement to be happy, you don't have to wait that long.

---

keep his business and has made much more of an impact than he would have had he sold it. You'll hear many such inspiring stories in this book.

My hope is that once you realize that you don't have to keep running toward an unrealistic finish line, you can find or keep doing work that fulfills you and makes you happy. This shift will reduce your stress about retirement; allow you to spend more of your time and money on yourself, your friends, and your family; and create space for a more fulfilling, balanced life.

Who This Book Is For

I began my career as a financial advisor in 1998. I have always taken a holistic approach toward developing financial plans with my clients. Early on, I worked with a few clients who were close to retirement, which gave me the opportunity to see firsthand that many of us may not be as happy as we expect when we take the traditional retirement route. I started asking my clients different questions than other financial advisors did, focusing more on what would bring satisfaction and happiness in addition to building a plan for their finances. I have over 50 long-term clients whom I've worked with for over 20 years—guiding them through life stages from raising young children to now working with some of their grown children.

After 25 years of financial advising, I can tell you that the majority of my clients do not walk into my office the first time we meet knowing that they don't want to retire. It takes a lot of exploration to confirm or deny if their current plan is right for them. Sometimes it is, but more often, it's not even close. My goal is to do the same thing for you: to help you clarify and build a plan around what works for *you*.

One of my philosophies is that we should be living our lives as if we are going to live another 100 years *and* as if we're going to die tomorrow. We should approach our financial situation in a way that allows us to enjoy the moment but also sets our future selves up for success and joy. This book will highlight the importance of the mix between the two.

If you are not currently saving enough for retirement, I empathize with you. At the same time, if you don't think your willingness or ability to save is going to change anytime soon, then traditional retirement will not come easily. This makes the approach in this book particularly relevant for you.

Conversely, the people I usually work with are initially saving too much and typically feel overwhelmed by their jobs. They constantly feel like they need to sacrifice short-term pleasure and relationships to set up a "better life" for themselves in the future. They may be working longer hours than ever before. Their marriages may be more strained than they've ever been. They may feel distant from their children or notice that their health and fitness are slipping. They do all of this in the name of being able to retire at 65.

In my practice, I noticed a pattern in who became serious about rethinking the future. Triggering events (i.e., big life changes) make people sit up and take a different approach to how they save. It isn't a hard-and-fast rule, but the most frequent triggering event is having children. Folks without kids can have just as much in assets but typically have less to worry about; they don't have the blessing/burden of planning for their children's college expenses and futures. A lot of my experience lies in helping people with families plan for their future, and you might notice a lot of examples and references including families.

But the approach in this book applies to everyone outside of that demographic too, as long as you have a desire and an intention to plan for your future. Other triggering events

Be open to the belief that there is a better solution than the one offered by the conventional path.

can and do happen to everyone: they include a death in the family and a resulting inheritance, an abrupt career change, or a divorce. If you've had a life event that has changed your outlook (for better or for worse), it's never too late to start planning for the future.

Sara Stibitz, the collaborative writer who helped me write this book, has a stark memory of the moment her mother, Karel, called her into the kitchen and told her, "Never depend on a man for money." Sara was 12 years old and didn't know why her mom gave her that advice until she pieced it together years later. It turned out that when her parents divorced, the reality of Karel's retirement prospects became terrifyingly clear. Sara's father had put money into retirement accounts with the intent that they would retire together, while they had spent everything Karel earned. When the relationship ended, he was kind enough to split the savings in half. But Karel was keenly aware that if it wasn't for his kindness, she would've been left with nothing.

Karel felt she had to work very hard to catch up. She worked a job she didn't love well into the evenings, which kept her away from Sara. She saved an incredible amount of money in a short time while laboring under the assumption that retirement happens at the age of 65. Unfortunately for Karel, she had a debilitating stroke at 53 and passed away at 59. She never got to use the money the way she intended.

Sara wonders what Karel's life would have been like—and what her own life would have been like—if Karel had decided to work beyond the age of traditional retirement so she could slow down, take care of her health, and spend time with her family. Karel is the perfect example of someone who had a major life change that made them realize they were not where they wanted to be. She didn't get the benefit of the guidance you'll find in this book, which could have helped her make the best decision for her.

Wherever you are in your journey, it's likely that you've consciously or unconsciously bought into the idea of traditional retirement and let it run the show behind the scenes. It affects the way you save and invest your money, spend your working days, and live your life. I want to get your attention and get you to realize, right now, that you probably won't ever stop working. At a minimum, I don't think you will want to stop entirely at 65. It's important to arrive at this conclusion as soon as you can instead of waiting to think about it when you are closer to traditional retirement.

Whether you feel you're ahead of the financial game; whether you feel you're behind; whether you're a nine-to-five employee, a business owner, or a trusted advisor; or whether you're just starting out in your career, the primary buy-in needed is an open mind to unconventional ideas. To get the most out of this book, you've got to be open to the belief that there is a better solution than the one offered by the conventional path. You'll have to get comfortable with or excited about the idea of working longer than the traditional retirement age. You'll have to get comfortable with the idea of doing something different from what society expects of you.

There's a common objection to this idea. Some people hate their jobs and don't want to do them any longer than necessary. I get it. But just because you hate your job doesn't mean that you'll love being jobless. The ideas in this book should help create a path for you to leave the job you hate and find work you enjoy.

I'm convinced that the way to find meaning and fulfillment and joy is to find something that you love doing, and then plan on doing it for a long time. There's one more layer to this, though: this book will likely work best for those who want to contribute to the world in a meaningful way. If your dream is to do nothing when you retire, this book probably isn't for you.

If this book alleviates even a fraction of your stress and anxiety around saving for retirement, I will have succeeded. I hope that what I have to share helps you realize that you can live a fulfilled and enjoyable life now *and* in the future. I hope to inspire and encourage you to reconsider what retirement looks like so you can spend more time and money on life-enriching experiences now, rather than pinching and saving for a version of retirement that you may not even enjoy.

RETHINKING RETIREMENT

{ 1 }

Retirement Is Not Working

YOU'RE PROBABLY facing one of two scenarios: You're either on pace to retire at the age you've chosen with the amount of money you want, or you're not.

Let's talk about the first scenario. If you're on track, you have the flexibility to look at your current job and ask yourself if you love doing it and if you want to continue doing it for the next 5, 10, or 20 years. If you don't enjoy your work, adopting a flexible mindset about retirement might enable you to transition out of that job earlier, especially if it demands a lot of hours and energy from you. You might even be able to make a small change, like going from 60 hours a week to 40 or 20 hours. Let me ask you something, though: Have you thought about what you may be sacrificing to stay on schedule?

Based on the statistics I shared in the introduction, it's more likely that you're not on track to retire. You might already be thinking about the sacrifices you'll have to make to reach your number or the sacrifices you'll have to make in retirement to live within your means. Planning to retire at 65 is—for most people and for many reasons—not feasible.

This is a tough realization, and I empathize with you. I want you to know that it's not your fault that you listened to what everyone told you about retirement. It's not your fault that you've felt forced to work hard and missed out on spending time with the people you love as a result. Some people might feel triggered by reading this book because they feel regret over how they've spent their time and money in the past decade. I want to acknowledge those feelings. It's okay to feel this way. These realizations can be tough to sit with, but recognizing them is the first step toward making meaningful changes. As I mentioned in the introduction, too many Americans haven't saved enough for traditional retirement. You are not alone.

No matter what track you're on, retiring at 65 is a hard-to-win battle. I've watched people hit their number by 65 by stressing, saving, and missing out on irreplaceable family time just to sock away money. When I first started working with clients, I noticed many felt way behind and imagined they would have to give up everything just to save. In both cases, they were forcing themselves to sacrifice vacations, time with family and friends, and their health and well-being for the sake of traditional retirement. I want to invite you to let that idea go and instead focus on how you might arrange your working life in a way that brings meaning and fulfillment so that you won't want to stop working.

A Tale of Two Tonys

Meet Tony, a 45-year-old professional earning $150,000 per year.[1] (Later I will introduce a calculator you can access to

Retirement is based almost entirely on opportunity costs: the cost of giving something up right now to have more in the future.

use your own income and savings inputs to personalize this example.)

Tony meets with a financial advisor to develop a retirement plan. He tells the advisor he is hoping to retire at 65 because that is the suggested age in all the articles he's read and the age that all his friends and colleagues are choosing to stop working. The advisor agrees this is a great choice, and they agree to meet again in two weeks to review the financial plan. Tony feels hopeful, as he has saved up $150,000 in his retirement account. However, that hope quickly fades when the advisor reveals that Tony is not on track. Far from it! In order to retire at 65, he would need to save an overwhelming 20 percent of his income, amounting to approximately $2,509 per month. With a young family, bills, and a mortgage to pay, as well as his desire to live some kind of enjoyable life, this figure is completely unrealistic and places a significant burden on his current financial situation. There is no way he can save that much given his current expenses, but he is determined to do whatever he can to get as close to that number as possible.

Tony begins working longer hours in the name of providing for his family, while he ironically spends less time with them. (This is a common excuse for many professionals to justify their absence around the house.) He gradually starts missing their nightly family dinners that were once sacred, and his eating habits begin to suffer because he only has time for fast food. They no longer go on their annual family vacation because Tony "can't afford to be away from the office for that long." He starts taking an antidepressant to help manage the stress and anxiety. Additionally, Tony lets his gym routine slide and skimps on his sleep.

Fast-forward 20 years. Despite making many sacrifices in order to retire, Tony didn't quite save enough to stop working. The good news for Tony is that he got pretty close to his number, and he is ironically not interested in retiring. He may decide to cut back the number of hours he works, but the idea of sitting around doing nothing for 30 years sounds miserable to him. The bad news is that Tony and his wife barely know each other anymore. His kids moved to the other side of the country, and he doesn't communicate with them much aside from a weekly phone call. If you were to look at his various investment accounts, you would see someone who is far from broke. If you were to bump into him on the street, you would see a broken man.

Have you seen *Sliding Doors*? It's a movie about a woman (played by Gwyneth Paltrow) whose love life and career hinge, unknown to her, on whether she makes it past the sliding door of a train she is hoping to catch. For our purposes, let's assume Tony has a sliding door moment that happens during a conversation he has with his wife a few days after the first meeting with the financial advisor.

Tony's wife asks him, "Why do you want to retire at 65? You seem to enjoy your job and coworkers. Even if you stop working at your current job, I can't imagine you will ever want to sit around and do nothing all day for 30 years. Maybe you'll figure out a way to turn your woodworking hobby into a business? If you did that, you won't ever want to fully stop. I mean, I am planning to reignite my career once the kids go off to college."

Tony begins to realize that he has no desire to ever completely stop working. He calls the financial advisor and tells him he doesn't think he wants to stop working at 65 and asks him to update the financial plan to show him new calculations under the assumption that he will work until he is 75. He might not always do what he is doing now, and he might not stop working then, but this feels more in line with how he expects his life to play out.

This extension dramatically alters his retirement plan. This time the financial advisor tells Tony that he only needs to save 1.5 percent of his income, or $175 per month, to meet his retirement goals.

Read that again. By extending his working years, Tony goes from having to save $2,509 per month, or 20 percent of his income, to saving $175, or 1.5 percent. The amount he needs to save for retirement is reduced by 93 percent.

Tony feels great about what was just presented to him! This amount, $175 per month, is far less than he is saving now. Without all the extra hours and extra stress he would have endured in the first scenario, Tony can continue to enjoy great balance and flexibility in his life. It's even more exciting that Tony now feels he can take some of the money that he would have had to save to make traditional retirement work and spend it on whatever he wants—experiences with his family, trips to bucket-list places, or improvements to his home and health.

Fast-forward 20 years, and Tony is getting ready to retire from his company. He rarely missed a family dinner, and he was one of the only people at his company who used up all his vacation time every single year. He and his wife have never been closer. And by the way, he isn't retiring because he wants to stop working. He is leaving his company because his online woodworking teaching business is thriving, and this will also allow him more time to visit his grandkids.

If Tony's wife had not asked a simple question that is shockingly rarely posed, Tony's life would have taken a much different course. By pausing to reflect and realize that he would likely want to work until 75, he struck a practical balance and created a much more fulfilling life for himself and those he loves.

When I share this scenario with clients and friends, they're both surprised and relieved by the fact that just a decade more of planned work could completely change the retirement game for them. By simply extending their savings time frames, the plan changes dramatically.

Your life doesn't have to play out like Tony's. Maybe you make more money than Tony. Maybe you make less. I share this comparison because I want you to see how planning to work longer can unlock an enormous amount of flexibility for your financial situation and life. Compound interest, extra contributions, and shifting cost/income ratios all work together to create an incredible impact on your savings when you lengthen your working years. But these exponential effects are nonintuitive, especially when planning over decades. That's why it's easy to overlook how changes like extending your working years and thus reducing the years you'll need to live off your investments can dramatically transform the feasibility of your financial plan.

As Tony learned, living a full life doesn't mean saving everything and forgoing the things that matter to you. Living a full life means enjoying life now *and* later.

The ROI of Right Now

The concept of retirement is based almost entirely on opportunity costs: the cost of giving something up right now in order to have more in the future. Opportunity cost is defined as the loss of potential gain from other alternatives when one alternative is chosen. We may decide not to spend $5,000 on a vacation right now because we believe that money will be worth more than $38,000 in 30 years (assuming a 7 percent annual rate of return on investing in the market). Most people choose to invest their money because it will likely be worth a lot more in the future than it is right now.

Generally, it's a good idea to invest money now instead of spending it so that you will have more of it in the future. This is a very good opportunity, and deferring unnecessary expenses will provide you with much more financial flexibility in the future. If you are like most people, this concept resonates, and you're willing to make the trade-off in many instances.

While most of us think often about the lost opportunity cost of not investing our money, I don't believe many of us think often about the lost opportunity costs of the experiences or happiness we defer when we focus almost exclusively on our long-term financial goals. It's true that the more you spend now, the harder it is to have what you will need in the future, especially if you are planning for a traditional retirement. However, it will be possible to earn more money in the future. But when it comes to experiences and relationships, the lost opportunity cost of time can never be recouped.

You might be making that trade-off—spending hours at work instead of with the people you love—with the idea that you'll have time later. But let me share a sobering idea with you. Tim Urban of the blog *Wait but Why* sketched out the number of days he'd spent with his family as compared to the number of days he could expect to spend with them in the future. He did the math and realized that by the time he graduated from high school, he had already spent 93 percent of his in-person time with his parents.[2] Even though he was only in his 30s, he was in the last 5 percent of time he had with them.

If you have kids, it's possible that you'll have spent 93 percent of your in-person time with them by the time they leave for college. I'll wait for you to grab a tissue. A dollar now is worth much more than a dollar in the future (inflation, etc.), and an hour with your spouse, or child, or on the golf course is worth way more now than it will be in 20 years. In fact, an hour now should significantly increase the odds of you getting more hours with them in the future.

When my first book, *Networking Is Not Working*, came out in 2014, I quickly started getting offers to speak on a lot of stages. At first, I was excited and flattered, but I remember the moment I started to question what I was doing. Three days after my book came out, an event organizer for a pet sitters' conference (yes, those exist) asked me to speak in Las Vegas. She offered to pay me to speak, and I immediately said yes.

Soon I found myself asking, *Do I really want to go to Vegas and speak to a bunch of pet sitters?* I wondered. I didn't have a course or anything to promote. There weren't any opportunities beyond a speaking fee. What stopped me more than anything else, though, was the thought of being away from my family. My sons were two and five years old at the time, and I'd already spent the previous year working longer hours just to get the book done. Did I really want to leave for three days for an amount of money that would make no difference to me in the long run? What kind of pattern would I set with that decision?

I stopped and thought about what kind of life I wanted, and time away on the road for speaking gigs wasn't part of my vision. At that moment, I adopted a mantra from my pastor, Mark Batterson, for myself: I want to be more famous in my home than I am anywhere else. And in order to do that, I needed to be at home a lot. So, with my tail between my legs, I went back to the event promoter and told her that it wasn't a good fit for me. That mantra has guided my decisions about how I live my life and what opportunities I take from that point on.

Fast-forward to the time when I started writing this book in 2017. I had a nice daily rhythm with my kids where I dropped them off at school in the morning, got my work done, and then spent time with them again in the afternoon and evening. They loved hanging out with me; there's no way they'd say no to an opportunity to hang with their dad. For those of you who are parents, you know this stage doesn't last forever.

We have to invest as much in our relationships as we do in our retirement accounts.

As kids get older, you can't pencil in time with them on the calendar. You have to be available and flexible enough so that you can be with them when they're ready to be with you. They start having friends and other interests that take up more of their time.

One day in 2021, I was just about to work out, and my oldest son said, "Hey, Dad, do you want to play LEGOs with me?" I said, "Hey, buddy, I would love to, but I'm getting ready to work out right now. I haven't done it in a couple of days, so I've got to get it in." In the middle of my workout, I froze, and thought to myself, *Oh my gosh, I don't want to ever say that to him again if I can help it. If he asks me to spend time with him, then I want to say yes.*

He was already at the age where most days he wasn't interested in hanging out with me. He was spending more time with his friends, playing games on his PlayStation, or doing homework. I realized that likely wasn't going to change for the better. So I rearranged my schedule so that I was more available for my kids when they were home, in case they *did* want to spend time together.

From that point on, I prioritized my days so that I completed everything that absolutely had to be done early in the day, including my workout. The tasks that would be nice to get done but weren't vitally important, I left for the afternoon. Most days, he did his own thing, and I finished my tasks. But at least two or three times a week, he asked me to play basketball or LEGOs, and I always had the time to say yes. The more I said yes, the more he asked. We got into a nice rhythm where we spent a lot of time together.

Two years later, my son is 14 and even less interested in spending time with me, except for a few things. We have a gym in our house, and he's gotten into working out. Three times a week, we work out together for an hour. He typically doesn't speak to me for 55 of those 60 minutes, but I'm in the game. Those five minutes are a good conversation, and he has a dad who's present and around so that if or when he has more to say, it's not going to be hard for him to reach me. We also use this time together to share new songs with each other. Music has been a great way for our family to bond.

In Ryan Holiday's *Daily Dad* blog, he shares the idea that there's no distinction between so-called quality time or garbage time when parenting. A lot of parents focus too much on trying to manufacture quality time—especially if they feel like they're always time-poor—when they should appreciate the time they have in the moment with their kids no matter what that moment looks like. I've come to realize that you can't just pencil kids in on the calendar and expect them to show up ready to engage. As kids get older, the time you have becomes more fleeting but potentially more meaningful. The key is building the ability to be present, with no expectations, into your schedule so that when they're ready, you're there.

In contrast, my relationship with my youngest son is incredible; he can't get enough of me right now, and we spend a lot of time together. I know this will end soon, and I keep that top of mind. Like any other parent, I get frustrated with the bedtime routine. I used to lie in bed with my son and wish he'd fall asleep a little faster so I could go have my glass of wine, watch TV, or spend time with my wife. After my older son started drifting away, I realized this would happen with my youngest too. So I transitioned to a place where I no longer wished those moments would end so I could go do something else. I had to work hard to feel grateful for the moment, but I knew I would miss those days when I was lying in bed with him at night. Whenever I thought about what I'd rather be doing, I focused on how I would feel 50 years from now if someone offered me the opportunity to go back in time and experience our old bedtime routine with the 10-year-old version of my son.

How much money would I pay for that chance? I'd easily pay $50,000 to go back in time and have one more nighttime snuggle with my kid. Even though it took me longer than I would have liked to get to this place, I've started treating these moments as $50,000 moments. How many $50,000 moments are you taking for granted in your life on a regular basis?

I've never once met someone who has said, "I think I maxed out the amount of time that I wanted to spend with my kids while they were growing up" or "I definitely didn't spend enough time at work when I was investing in other relationships." I like following the model that my father set: being a dad and a husband before anything else. It has meant the world to me to decide that I will continue to work in order to have quality time with my family and my close friends now and later, the same way that my dad did.

One of my North Stars is that I want to live my life in a way that will increase the likelihood that my children will want to spend more time with me when they're adults. That's how I make a lot of my choices and decisions right now. I do all of this without any guilt or feeling that there will be consequences in the future for not working harder. I work and make less than a lot of my contemporaries because I spend more time with my family and friends.

This lifestyle is sponsored by the fact that I know without a shadow of a doubt that I'm going to work until the day I pass away. Knowing that I have no interest in sitting around in retirement affords me the flexibility and the freedom to live my life the way I want to now, as I have been for the past 5 or 10 years. I actually feel I'm going to be ready to sign up for 60-to-70-hour workweeks again once my youngest heads off to college. I'm going to be ready to speak on more stages and take on more opportunities to serve and work with people. I believe that in my core.

I may even head to Vegas in 2028 for the pet sitters' conference. They seem like the type of people who likely won't ever want to stop what they are doing.

The choice to change the way you think about work and retirement comes down to quality of life and the opportunity to spend time with the people you love now rather than waiting until you have all the money in the world to retire. If you have children, would they rather you spend more time with them while they are 10 or when they are 40? If you are married, would your spouse prefer monthly date nights and quarterly getaways right now versus minimal romance now and playing catch-up later in life? Do you think your friends will wait around for 20 years while you spend your life at work to save for traditional retirement, when you could be planning that vineyard tour or golf trip in Europe for next April?

Speaking of friends, when most people looked at the graph below—which shows who Americans spend their time with by age—they noticed the dramatic increase in alone time as we get older more than they notice anything else.[3]

The corresponding advice that accompanied this revelation from folks who were sharing the image online suggested that we need to get more comfortable being alone since we'll be spending so much time by ourselves as we age.

Why are we accepting this idea that our later years will be filled with massive amounts of alone time?

What sticks out most to me is the decline of time spent with friends as we get older.

Between 2009 and 2019, the average 15-year-old spent over 100 minutes a day with friends and only about 200 minutes alone. Fast-forward to age 30 and, as the data suggests, the average person spends more time with their coworkers

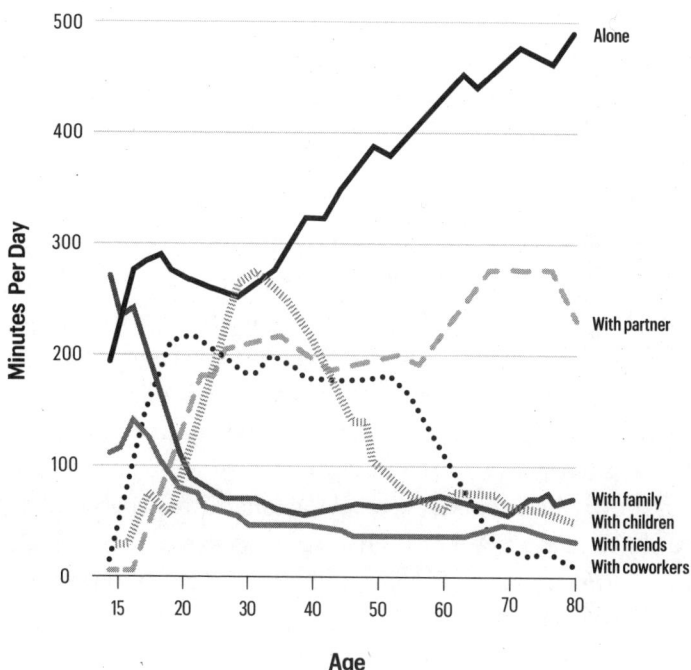

Relationships used to categorize people are not exhaustive. Additionally, time spent with multiple people can be counted more than once (e.g., attending a party with friends and a partner counts toward both "friends" and "partner").

Source: ourworldindata.org/time-use

than with family, and a little over 50 minutes per day with friends against 250 minutes alone. By the age of 50, we spend less than 30 minutes per day with friends on average and more than 350 minutes alone.

When did we begin to devalue the importance of friendship? Our lives revolved around our friends and having a good time in our formative years. As adults, we easily forgo time with friends in favor of work and other obligations, which I don't think we should accept. Quality friendships are an important part of a fulfilling life, but if we want to maintain our connections, we need to act now. We have to invest as much in our relationships as we do in our retirement accounts (we'll talk more about this later in the book).

I'd like you to consider the $5,000 vacation I mentioned above. Let's say you decided that it would be unwise to spend that money on time with your children while they were young (10, 8, and 5) or to take that blowout vacation with your friends, and invested it instead. Now, 30 years later, you're 70, and your children are grown or your friends have drifted away. Everyone has their own lives, and they don't have time to hang out with you the way you envisioned. Your spouse has grown distant because of all the long nights you spent at work. You have saved enough to retire and are thinking back to this time in your life and wondering if it was a mistake to skip a vacation that year.

Lucky for you, there's still time to create a new North Star for yourself. This is an opportunity to change your trajectory, create a different financial plan, and build a more fulfilling life.

{ 2 }

How We Got Here: The History of Retirement

BELIEVE IT or not, the concept of retirement is barely a hundred years old. Younger still is the idea of retirement as a major life goal, something you worked and saved toward. Most people did not live long enough to have a retirement; they worked until they died. The first retirement program was created to provide for the handful of people who were lucky enough to outlive their ability to work. Unsurprisingly, it was created by a conservative politician in response to pressure from the opposing party.

The Invention of Retirement

In 1883, the conservative minister and chancellor of the German Empire, Otto von Bismarck, felt threatened by the Marxists trying to take control of Europe. He wanted to make sure that his people were cared for while keeping his socialist opposition at bay, so he designed a government-run system to financially support the older citizens of his country. As articulated by Germany's emperor in a letter to parliament: "Those who are disabled from work by age and invalidity have a well-grounded claim to care from the state."[1] Six years later, in 1889, the world's first old-age social insurance program went into effect.

When Bismarck designed the German program, he selected the age of 70 as the age of retirement because that was the age to which Germans were generally expected to live. Read that again. It wasn't until 27 years later that the "retirement" age for Germans was lowered to 65.[2]

Meanwhile, the US faced big problems too. Before the US Social Security Administration was created in 1935, unemployment was rampant, especially among younger workers. At the same time, the concept of retirement didn't really exist. Older workers wanted to continue working to support themselves, holding on to their jobs until they could physically no longer work or until they died. This created a gap in opportunity for younger workers that harshly impacted the economy. What's more, older workers—particularly those in factory settings—made mistakes that cost companies money.

The resulting ageism was so rampant that as soon as their hair started showing the first signs of gray, men bought shoe polish to cover it, a practice they had to keep up every day.[3] Visible signs of aging served as a sign of decreased speed and agility. Those older men were then transferred to harder jobs that were even more difficult to keep up with, and once they failed, their employer had every reason to fire them.[4] As we all know, a sense of personal power, camaraderie, and connection are so important, as well as the sense of ability to provide. Losing your job was a devastating event. No one wanted to sit around waiting for their children to provide for them.

One of the major reasons for the creation of retirement plans, pension plans, and Social Security programs was to move older people out of the workforce. As the management of the Pennsylvania Railroad put it, the pension system permitted the company to humanely get rid of any drones who encumbered the work and to keep the entire staff "fresh."[5] Basically, pension plans gave them an easy way to put people out to pasture and bring in new people who could do the jobs better and faster. The younger men consistently got much more work done than the older men, who pleaded with them to slow down and take their time.[6]

To keep their morale up, the men who were pushed out of work formed clubs.[7] Most people opted not to move in with their children because they didn't want to be a burden to them, even though that made it more likely they would be unable to pay for their homes. I think this is where we get the belief that we have to work as hard as possible and bend over backward when we're ordered to do something. It comes from the generational fear that if you don't, won't, or can't do it, someone else will—and you'll be fired. No wonder so many of us have made our entire lives about our jobs, pouring everything we have into them, leaving little left for anything else.

In 1933, physician-turned-activist Francis Townsend wrote a letter to his local newspaper proposing a mandatory retirement age of 60 with the intention of creating a way for older workers to comfortably stop working. The Townsend Plan quickly gained popularity and support. Among other things, it proposed that the government would pay those who retired $200 per month, which in some cases was more than they had earned while working.[8]

The idea was generous—too generous. It didn't go over well with politicians *or* laborers. Everyone would have received the monthly stipend, even seniors who had never worked before—in many ways, it was like an early version of the concept of universal basic income. Those who received the money would be required to spend the entire amount and put it back into the economy; they couldn't save any of it. These people were already living paycheck to paycheck, so being forced to put everything back into the economy didn't sit well with them. It also had the feel of a "handout," and the men who had worked their entire lives didn't like that idea, so the Townsend Plan went nowhere.

Enter Social Security

When US president Franklin D. Roosevelt proposed the Social Security Act, which stipulated that workers would pay for their own old-age insurance, people liked the concept because they would contribute to it and withdraw their "own money."

There's a story about the first person who ever received Social Security that highlights the most important part about these funds. Even though the Social Security Act was established in 1935, they had to let it run for five years before anyone could take any money out. In January 1940, Ida May Fuller drew the first Social Security check, for $22.54.[9] She was a retired legal secretary and started drawing benefits at the age of 65 after contributing for about five years. Well, she blew right by the actuarial tables and kept receiving monthly checks until she died—at age 100. Because she had contributed for so little time, her contribution prior to retiring was only $24.75. Care to guess how much she drew over the rest of her life? A whopping $22,889.[10]

This is a painfully poignant example of how Social Security, right from the beginning, wasn't set up to be sustainable. It

Wherever you land on the generational map, it's clear the old concept of retirement needs a rethink.

was meant to bridge the gap years between pensions and savings and your eventual death. When we live for 20 or 30 years beyond the point where we stop working, what we have in Social Security will be nowhere near enough to allow us to replace a significant portion of our salary. And when a whole nation lives far beyond their expected years...

For the most part, I try to refrain from offering advice around political issues, but it might be obvious by now where I stand on the topic of Social Security. Given the original intention of the program, the fact that it was only set up to provide income for a short amount of time as opposed to decades, and that many of the people who were supposed to benefit in the early days died before they could even reap the benefits of it, I don't think it's sound to rely on any kind of Social Security income—especially for those who are under the age of 50. The bottom line is that if we keep living longer, then the benefits are going to have to extend longer.

True, part of our problems with Social Security will resolve themselves because we have fewer workers now than we did 30 years ago, and our birth rate is on the decline, but there are still fundamental issues with the program that make it a questionable asset to rely on. No matter how you feel about it, most of the research suggests the funds will run out by 2030.

Private Pension Plans and 401(k)s

Decades before Social Security was put in place, American Express was the first to offer a private pension to employees, in 1875.[11] In the 1920s, more companies began to do the same. From 1940 to the 1960s, the number of people covered by pension plans increased by a factor of five, going from 3.7 million to 19 million, almost 30 percent of the labor force. By 1975, pension plans had reached their pinnacle, covering 40 million people.[12]

By the 1960s, the burden of paying for employees to retire had become too onerous, and one by one, the plans started to collapse. The first to collapse was Studebaker, an automobile manufacturer. The company had been on the edge of bankruptcy for years when it closed its South Bend, Indiana, plant in 1963. Shortly after the shutdown, the company ended the retirement plan for hourly workers, and the fund defaulted on its obligations.[13]

A decade later, after many other companies had defaulted on their pension obligations to their employees, the Employee Retirement Income Security Act (ERISA) of 1974 passed with a provision that left employers liable should they slip on their fiduciary duties.[14] They could now be sued for restitution, which meant the burden was even greater to manage the pension plans more responsibly. Offering a pension plan was becoming a hassle for employers.

Today, traditional pension plans are mostly a thing of the past. They're almost non-existent aside from those offered by government employers and some law firms. Only 15 percent of private industry workers had access to one in 2022, according to the US Bureau of Labor Statistics.[15] Even government pensions are becoming too burdensome for many states to pay out after their employees retire.

Four years after ERISA, US Congress passed the Revenue Act of 1978, which included a provision that gave workers a tax-free way to defer compensation for bonuses or stock options. This was a way for companies to offer something meaningful for their employees, something other than a pension. They could offer tax-advantaged savings to their employees while removing themselves from the burden of having to manage the money and ensure that the defined benefit would be intact when people retired. With these new contribution plans, they could share the responsibility with their employees.

When the Internal Revenue Service (IRS) issued new rules that allowed employees to contribute to their 401(k) plans through salary deductions in 1981, the retirement planning industry experienced a healthy jump-start and has only grown from there. Just look at the numbers for 401(k) plans from 1990 to 2023:

- 1990: 19 million active participants, with over $384 billion in assets[16]

- 1996: 30 million active participants, with over $1 trillion in assets[17]

- 2023: 70 million active participants, with over $7.4 trillion in assets[18]

But it isn't all sunshine and roses. You may be surprised to hear that the original creators and supporters of these plans are dismayed by their widespread use. Ted Benna, widely regarded as the father of the 401(k), has said with some regret that he "helped open the door for Wall Street to make even more money than they were already making"[19] and that he knew "it was going to be big, but I was certainly not anticipating that it would be the primary way people would be accumulating money for retirement 30 plus years later."[20] Possibly more alarming is his claim that the plan was never meant to be what it is today.

Naysayers of the plan abound. Early backers of the plan acknowledge that it was never meant to be a primary retirement tool and that forecasts in the early days were too optimistic.[21] From the 2000s to today, two recessions and periodic market declines have exposed all of us to retirement savings volatility. Still others say that the abundance of 401(k) plans has exposed workers-turned-investors to drops and fluctuations of the stock market they weren't prepared for or expecting, not to mention the high fees of the money managers. More than a few people have watched in horror as their savings were cut in half because they were still exposed to risk despite being close to retirement. However, the returns of the stock market over the past 50 years have been net positive for the majority of its participants.

The Reality of Retirement Today

Retirement has slowly become less attainable for everyone. Boomers are now retiring at record levels but have deep concerns about health-care costs and income longevity. A 2023 Vanguard study shows that for individuals aged 65 and older, the median 401(k) balance is $70,620.[22] Once they reach the age of 65, females can expect to live to 86 years old, and males to 83.[23] This increasing life expectancy means most people's 401(k) savings are far below the levels needed to fund 20-plus years of retirement. Given our low savings rates and long lifespans, it might be no surprise that people who are 65 and older represent one of the fastest-growing demographics of the workforce.[24] Projections indicate that by 2032, one in four US workers will be 55 years of age or older; almost one in ten will be 65 or older. And 27 percent of Americans aged 65 to 74 are actively looking for work.[25]

As of this writing, more and more folks are "unretiring." In one Harvard study, researchers spoke to retirees about what they missed about working. The number one response was the social connections at work that had given them so much fulfillment.[26] Another study showed that often, people leave retirement for emotional reasons as much as for financial

Today, retirees who stop working at age 65 need to have enough money to last 25 years or more.

reasons. People who retired early told researchers that the transition into retired life—in other words, not working—was less relaxing than they'd hoped. "It is perfectly normal to discover that life post-financial freedom isn't as happy as one might have expected it to be," the researchers reported.[27] Retirees faced challenges like carving out new identities and directions in life and dealing with sadness, isolation, and a lack of meaning in their day-to-day lives.[28] In 2024, one in eight retired people planned to go back to work because of insufficient savings, high costs due to inflation, and boredom.[29] I was speaking with a client recently who told me they ran into an old professional friend at Home Depot. They had done a lot of business together over the years and were members of the same country club. Just as he noticed the orange apron around his old friend, he realized it had been a while since he had seen him on the golf course. In anticipation of an awkward silence, his friend quickly volunteered that he had to get a job because he had retired too soon. Unfortunately, this sort of thing is happening far too often. People are retiring from their jobs because they think they have enough without properly accounting for all the uncertainties that have the potential to disrupt their plan.

Millennials are notably behind as compared to other generations. Millennials hold 5 percent of the nation's wealth; when Baby Boomers were the same age, they held 21 percent.[30] Where 45 percent of Gen X and Baby Boomers participated in their workplace retirement options by the age of 31, only 33 percent of Millennials did.[31] Making matters worse, Millennials hold more student debt. Millennials are part of the biggest demographic of the Financial Independence, Retire Early (FIRE) movement. While that doesn't mean all of them will actually retire, it does mean more and more workers are looking for nontraditional work arrangements.

Gen Z is still focused on building financial stability. The members of this generation (as well as most Millennials) are deeply skeptical that Social Security will exist in the future—rightfully so—and see a need to either completely self-fund their retirement or plan not to exit the workforce. Gen Z seems to hope that by saving for retirement sooner, they will be able to retire earlier. From a financial industry perspective, saving sooner isn't a bad idea, but it seems to indicate that Gen Z has bought into the idea that they won't love their jobs and they should try to remove themselves from work as soon as possible.

Among all generations, there's an increasing belief that ending work will put them out of misery sooner (look at the FIRE movement, for example). I believe that people don't even know it's possible to create a life—which includes fulfilling work—that they don't have to retire from.

Whenever I meet someone who declares, "I'm going to retire at 45," I feel bad for them. They usually come across as proud for having a game plan to exit the workforce before their peers, but I can't imagine disliking how I spend 40 hours of my week so much that I need to aggressively work to escape it as soon as possible by assuredly forgoing a more pleasurable life right now. When you buy into the concept of retirement, you are likely buying into a few other things, even if at a subconscious level. You are probably buying into the belief that your life will be better in the future than it is now. You are probably buying into the belief that all work is a means to an end and something you must endure now to be happy in the future. Why not at least try to find work that you enjoy and that you won't want to retire from?

Wherever you land on the generational map, it's clear the old concept of retirement needs a rethink. For younger generations, this optimistic idea of "traditional" retirement at 65 is unlikely—and you're better off if you take it into your own hands and define it for yourself.

What This Means for You

Retirement was never meant to be a stage of life where you did nothing but sit around on your front porch drinking lemonade for 30 years. It was created to help older workers in the last few years of their lives and to open job opportunities for the youngest generations who were just entering the workforce.

The age of retirement was chosen to serve the needs of a program for which 60 was too early and 70 was too late, and yet everyone still identifies with it almost a hundred years later, despite the fact that life expectancy has increased dramatically.

Back then, if a worker retired at 65, average life expectancy statistics predicted they would live for another seven years. The retiree could count on a third of their income from Social Security, and another third from their company pension. They only had to come up with a third of their living expenses, and only needed to do so for an average of seven years.

Today, retirees who stop working at age 65 need to have enough money to last 25 years or more. What's more, Social Security income accounts for very little of a typical retiree's living expenses, and with the collapse of pension plans, they need to come up with the rest of the funds themselves. To retire fully at 65 today, we need to come up with close to 100 percent of our retirement savings on our own, and to top it off, we need enough to provide for ourselves for 25 or maybe 30 years or more in some cases.

That's a tall order. When you consider it, and the fact that those who fully retire typically experience declines in health, emotional well-being, and life satisfaction, the case for full retirement doesn't add up.

{ 3 }

Happiness versus Meaning

YOU MIGHT feel entitled to a break if you've been working a job you hate, grinding it out for years or even decades. You might be thinking you just worked this job for most of your life; missed out on time with your kids, your partner, and your buddies; and put off trips with family just to feed them. And you might feel like that was so stressful that you're entitled to do nothing for the next 30 years of your life. If that's your current situation, then I'm sure retirement sounds glorious to you.

If you feel undervalued or that you are doing work that does not bring you or others value, I will never encourage you to do it one day longer than you need to. Under those circumstances, you might even find that retirement makes you happy for a short period of time, but I don't think it will provide you with lasting happiness. One of the primary reasons I want you to consider forgoing a traditional retirement is because you will live a far better life with meaningful work—now and in the future.

However, happiness is often difficult to achieve when it is the primary goal. This Wayne Dyer story highlights what I mean.

> There was an old wise cat and a small kitten in an alleyway. The old cat saw the kitten chasing its tail and asked, "Why are you chasing your tail?"
>
> The kitten replied, "I've been attending cat philosophy school, and I have learned that the most important thing for a cat is happiness, and that happiness is located in my tail. Therefore, I am chasing it: and when I catch it, I shall have happiness forever."
>
> Laughing, the wise old cat replied, "My son, I wasn't lucky enough to go to cat philosophy school, but as I've gone through life, I too have realized that the most important thing for a cat is happiness, and indeed that it is located in my tail. The difference I've found though is that whenever I chase after it, it keeps running away from me, but when I go about my business and live my life, it just seems to follow after me wherever I go."[1]

As Dyer so eloquently illustrates, I don't think you will be happier by pursuing happiness.

Happiness or Meaning?

If you could be doing anything right now, anywhere in the world, what would make you happy? You may be thinking to yourself that sipping a fruity, alcoholic beverage on a beach in Hawaii cannot be topped. While that sounds amazing, I don't think it will make you happier than spending some time in a flow state.

Mihaly Csikszentmihalyi, the Hungarian American psychologist who studied many important psychological concepts, interviewed over 8,000 people from different walks of life: "from Dominican monks, to blind nuns, to Himalayan climbers, to Navajo shepherds."[2] His research concluded that when people are engaged in meaningful work, they feel more content and satisfied with their lives. He found that when people are fully absorbed in the task at hand, they are at their happiest, and the feeling is even more enhanced when the activity is just the right amount of challenging. He described that experience as "flow": a "state in which people are so involved in an activity that nothing else seems to matter; the experience is so enjoyable that people will continue to do it even at great cost, for the sheer sake of doing it."[3]

For that kind of flow state to occur, people must see the activity as voluntary and enjoyable, and the work must require enough skill and challenge with clear goals toward success. He also found that when people feel they have control over the activity, and they receive immediate feedback, they are far more likely to enjoy their work.[4]

Notice that he did *not* say that people are happiest when they are sitting on the couch binge-watching the latest, greatest TV show just because they can or when they have no responsibility.

With that in mind, do you want to be happy? Or do you want your life to have meaning? Yes, this is a trick question.

Meaningful Medicine

Not buying it? If you don't want to take the vitamins I'm offering, then I'm going to give you some medicine.

We've all heard of studies that show that happiness is good for the body. Happy minds and healthy bodies have been shown to be linked when it comes to positive health outcomes. But newer studies seem to call this into question by diving deeper into the meaning of "happiness" and what it means for our health. It turns out that pursuing happiness might not be as good for the body as we thought.

In one study, researchers dug into the difference between what we mean when we use the word "happiness" and the difference between having a happy life and a meaningful life. They found that happiness is associated with taking behavior, while having a sense of meaning is associated with giving.[5] Feeling happy is connected to feeling good personally, but feeling that your life is meaningful is connected to serving others.[6] The lead researcher noted, "Partly what we do as human beings is to take care of others and contribute to others. This makes life meaningful, but it does not necessarily make us happy."[7]

Adam Grant supports this idea in his book *Give and Take*, in which he talks about a variety of scenarios highlighting the differences between people who are givers and people who are takers. The people who prioritize happiness are often the takers, meaning they're typically focused on their own happiness more than the happiness of others. Meanwhile, those who are focused on giving to other people feel they have more meaning in their lives. Just to be clear, I am not referring to giving in the purely altruistic sense, although that can apply. The giving I am referring to—your wisdom, your gifts, your experience—always generates some type of return, usually a monetary one.

Yet another study delves even further into what this means on a cellular level. Researchers looked at the self-reported levels of happiness and meaning in 80 subjects, using the same definitions in the previous study.[8] As before, happiness was defined as "feeling good personally." They asked the participants questions about the frequency of feeling happy, their interest in life, and how often they felt satisfied. The more

What makes you happy in the short term isn't likely to give you meaning in the long term.

strongly people responded, the higher they scored on happiness. Likewise, meaning in life was defined as "an orientation to something bigger than the self." They asked questions to gauge whether and how often they felt a sense of direction or purpose in their lives, how often they felt they had something to contribute to society, and whether they felt a sense of belonging in a community.

After the subjects submitted their answers, researchers then examined their individual gene expression. Their hope was to see how a subject's feeling of happiness or meaning influenced their gene expression. They found that people who scored high for happiness but low for meaning have "the same gene expressions as people who are responding to and enduring chronic adversity."[9]

Previous work has linked chronic adversity to poor health. For example, when people are lonely or dealing with particularly challenging life circumstances (like loss of a loved one, loss of a job, etc.), their bodies are in a constant state of threat.[10] This sets off the expression of a stress-related gene pattern that has negative effects: a higher number of proinflammatory genes and a decrease of the activity of genes involved in antiviral responses.[11] In other words, research shows that people who are happy but have little to no sense of meaning and are just here for the party have gene expression patterns similar to people enduring chronic adversity. People who have a strong sense of meaning show a deactivation of the adversity response, meaning their bodies are not preparing them for bacterial infections, and their inflammation is not increasing.

This is a roundabout way of saying that when you're serving other people, when your life is oriented toward the good of something greater than yourself, you are fostering and facilitating strong social bonds, which leads to lower inflammation and rates of disease. When you're just here to serve yourself, you are far more likely to experience high inflammation, which eventually leads to disease and poor health.

Let me ask you this: If you don't love your work, why not? Is it a lack of meaning in the day-to-day work you do or even the big picture goals? Is it because no matter how meaningful the work is, you just don't like it? Or is it that the environment is terrible? And if it's the environment, is it the company itself or is it the people who surround you that make your work less than desirable? The way you answer this question will shed some light on the best option for improving your situation.

We're all here to accomplish something, and if your only goal is to be happy, then you're missing the point. What makes you happy in the short term isn't likely to give you meaning in the long term. If you think you'll be happy sipping fruity drinks on the beach, you will—but only for a week or so. If you did that every day with no end in sight, you'd get bored. Maybe even within a year. However, if you continue making contributions to society, to have or find meaning in your life, you might just find something that is far better than happiness.

Health and Longevity

People often worry about not being able to work. What if they decide they'll work past 65 and then fall ill, and then because they didn't pinch and save, they don't have enough money? This is a valid concern. Another corresponding fear is centered on the possibility that you will far outlive the money you earned. Both come into play when thinking about your future, so you want to make sure you are protected in these scenarios.

We'll dive deeper into this later, but for now, I will address how you can best prepare for these unforeseen and unlikely events. Let's say something happens to you five years from now, and you're not able to enjoy the same lifestyle. Will you look back on that and think, *I'm glad I spent the last five years working my butt off and didn't take time to travel or spend more time with my family*, or will you be glad that you did those things while you were able to? If you have the right plan in place, which includes some insurance to protect you against unexpected events, your bills are going to continue to get paid—but there's no way to get that lost time back.

Dr. Peter Attia touches on this when he talks about longevity. He says that you should pursue longevity, not so that you can live to 100 instead of 91, but so you can improve your health span and the quality of your life while you reach the end of it.[12] Director of the Institute of Inflammation and Ageing at the University of Birmingham Janet Lord says, "This is not about developing the first 1,000-year-old human; it's about ensuring old age is enjoyed and not endured. Who wants to extend lifespan if all that means is another 30 years of ill health? This is about increasing health span, not lifespan."[13]

Most longevity or health advice focuses on the payoff that comes 20 years from now; the central theme of this book is that I want you to feel good about life now and later—not just put off fulfillment.

Building good health habits now will beget good health later: both in 20 years and in two hours. It's amazing how much easier it is to feel motivated and to enjoy your work and your family when you feel good physically. The more time you put aside to take care of yourself, the more you will take care of yourself.

A Challenge

One way I gauge whether prospective clients truly love what they're doing is to ask them to imagine they won $50 million in the lottery. I want you to do the same now. If you won the lottery and never had to work again, how would your life change?

This exercise provides clarity on two key things: First, it should reveal whether you are currently doing work you truly love. There are people who would continue the same work regardless of money. If that's you, congratulations—most don't feel that way. If not, finding fulfilling work is something to aspire to.

Second, if you were suddenly financially liberated, which relationships or experiences would you pursue? In other words, what are you putting off right now because you don't have that freedom, and how would that change if you could do whatever you wanted? If you are putting those things off now with the intention of doing them in the future, will the quality of the experience be diminished by waiting 10 or 30 years?

This ties into two other revealing questions I ask new clients: If a doctor told you that you had one year left to live, how would you spend that year? And if they said you were going to die tomorrow, what would your biggest regret be?

These questions help determine if you're doing work you truly love right now, or if there's another type of work you'd rather pursue. They also uncover experiences and relationships you deferred that either money would solve or that you might prioritize if time was extremely limited.

If you are one of the many people who believe you have to work a job you do not enjoy for a long time to earn the right to be happy, I am sorry. If you believe you do not deserve to enjoy your life until you have earned your keep, I am sorry. If

You weren't put on this planet to work really hard in a job you hate for 30 years so you can sit around and do nothing for another 30 years after that.

you believe that no longer having to do something that you disliked for most of your life will suddenly make you happy, I am sorry. Remember, it's not your fault that you've been sold the idea of traditional retirement that forces you into saving aggressively to live the life you want "someday."

If you don't like what you do right now, you are probably upset with me for even suggesting that you do it for longer than what you are expecting. If you don't like what you do right now, I don't want you to continue to do it. Now you may have to continue that work for the near future because of various obligations; however, I want to highlight that you weren't put on this planet to work really hard in a job you hate for 30 years so you can sit around and do nothing for another 30 years after that.

Living a meaningful life isn't all about you—it's about what you contribute to the people around you. And it isn't necessarily related to some grand purpose or career. Not everyone needs to seek out a life-defining purpose through their work. The idea that everyone must find their passion or purpose in their job can be misleading. Instead, we should focus on where we already find satisfaction in our roles and expand on that fulfillment as much as possible. This shift in perspective is crucial. For many, their calling might be organizing monthly gatherings for their friends or volunteering in their communities to help others. You have gifts, wisdom, and experiences to share with the world, and we need these from you!

In that light, a day-to-day job can serve as a means to an end, supporting meaningful activities—however you define them. My brother-in-law has a friend who is a computer programmer. He keeps this job solely to support his love for attending Phish concerts. He doesn't hate his job; he likes the people he works with and the work itself well enough, although he doesn't have any fantasies about doing it forever. The job gives him the opportunity to use his skills to earn money in a way that supports the life he wants to live. It's crucial to point out, though, that his job doesn't stress him out to the point where he's too tired to see the live music he loves.

If you are not happy with your current work situation, I am going to assume it is trickling into other areas of your life. If you dislike what you do for a living, it is almost certainly having a negative effect on your mindset, health, and relationships. I don't want you to do something you don't enjoy any longer than is necessary, and I also don't want you to delay experiencing peace, joy, and fulfillment. I want you to be fulfilled in 20 years, and I want you to feel amazing right now. I want you to leave your crappy job and find work that is better suited for you, to ultimately engage in work that you find intriguing, fulfilling, and endlessly worthwhile. In the upcoming chapters, I am going to provide you with strategies and options to make this a reality.

{ 4 }

The Questions You Need to Be Asking

IF YOU ARE under the age of 60 and you tell me you know exactly what you want your life to look like when you're 75, I'm going to tell you that you're wrong. I don't know exactly how your life will evolve and neither do you. One of my favorite books is *Stumbling on Happiness* by Harvard professor Daniel Gilbert, which explores the idea that we all do a terrible job of predicting what will make our future selves happy. Most of us have bought into the idea that retiring someday will make us happy. And that when we retire, we will be happier than we are now because of the sacrifices we make.

I've seen this play out again and again with my clients. There are so many variables that will come into play, and correctly assuming all of them would be akin to winning the lottery. However, the financial industry assumes you can predict your desires or circumstances 10, 20, or 30 years from now. This prediction determines your "number," the "correct" amount needed for retirement. If you've had conversations about retirement with your coworkers, friends, or family, you have likely heard people share their number, or ask about yours. Your number is the total amount of money you will need to be financially independent. It is the lump sum amount that will allow you to stop working. One could argue that the primary purpose of traditional retirement planning is to help folks determine this number.

The problem with calculating your number is that you have to make a lot of assumptions by asking questions that are difficult (if not impossible) to answer, such as the following:

- What age do you want to retire?
- How much will you spend in retirement?
- How much are you planning to add to your investments going forward (monthly, annually, etc.)? Will this number increase or decrease over time?
- Do you plan on receiving Social Security benefits?
- What will the inflation rate be every year?
- What tax rates will you assume going forward?
- What age will you (and your spouse, if married) die?
- Do you want to leave money behind as a legacy (for grandchildren, or for charitable causes) or do you want to spend the money down?
- How much risk is appropriate for your investments during your working years (what rate of return will you assume)?
- How much risk is appropriate for your investments after you retire (what rate of return will you assume)?

How could you, or anyone, possibly know the exact answers to all these questions?

In this chapter, we're going to call into question the validity of the assumptions of the financial industry, and we'll talk about how the slightest change to any one of your assumptions will create wildly different plans and outcomes. We'll highlight how ridiculous it is to assume that you'll know what you want (or even who you'll be) in 10 years, let alone in 30 years.

And faced with all that, we'll make the case that the only reliable source of flexibility and freedom will be your ability to gainfully earn an income for a longer period.

How Accurate Is Your Crystal Ball?

If you have ever met with a financial professional, they almost certainly did not ask you, "Do you want to retire?" Or "Do you want to slow down at some point?" The idea of living a life you love right now that includes doing work you enjoy and never want to retire from is a foreign concept to most people. Working beyond the traditional retirement age is certainly not an option presented to you by the financial services industry. Instead, financial professionals are asking, "What age do you want to retire?" And when they ask that question, most people aren't really sure how to answer. If you admit to your uncertainty, they will suggest that you, like everyone else, will probably want to stop working at 65. I mean, it was the age Otto von Bismarck deemed to be appropriate over a hundred years ago. Not to mention the fact that it's good for their business if you aim to retire at 65—the more money you need to invest, the more money they make.

Be honest: If you previously determined what age you want to retire, is it because you gave it a lot of thought, or because you went along with what seemed like a good suggestion from someone else?

Even if you feel great about your chosen retirement age, this is only the first step of many in determining how much money you will need by that age.

After you consider your age of retirement, the next primary data point you need to calculate your number is the amount of money you think you'll spend in retirement. Truthfully, there's only one correct answer: "I have absolutely no idea." Since this is the case for most of us, the financial services industry (once again) has given us some suggestions.

Based on best practices from the industry, most financial institutions will tell you that you should plan on having 70 percent of your yearly income to live comfortably in retirement. This is primarily based on two assumptions: that you will have a simpler lifestyle in retirement than you do now, and that you won't spend the portion of your income that you have been investing for retirement once you stop working.

The only people I know who have a reduced lifestyle in retirement compared to what they enjoyed during their working years are those who have to, not because they want to. Suggesting that you will have a simpler life when you are older seems motivated by a desire to make you feel like retirement is more attainable than it is. I always ask my clients, "Do you typically spend more money on Mondays or Saturdays?" No one has ever said Mondays. We're all too busy at work. Traditional retirement is Saturday every day.

I don't think that you're going to be spending less in retirement. You'll have the potential to spend more, and you should. If anything, most people I know who participate in the traditional retirement planning model are putting off the pleasures of life right now because they need to save more of their money so they can eventually stop working. If you are doing this now, I can make an argument that you will want to spend more money in the future on the things you enjoy compared to today. This brings us to the second assumption.

The answer isn't "just work harder, longer hours." The answer is to change the way you think about retirement.

If someone invests 30 percent of their current income and enjoys a lifestyle with the remaining 70 percent, and that lifestyle is unlikely to change, then the math can work. However, it is unlikely you are setting aside 30 percent of your current income. Don't feel bad, though. Hardly anyone is able to live the way they want to live by spending less than 50 percent of their income after taxes. About 10 percent of my clients live this much beneath their means. One client makes $1 million per year and spends about $250,000 annually. He and his family have been in the same house for 30 years and have no intention of moving. They live a relatively modest, simple lifestyle and give away a lot of their money. That client is a rare example of somebody who will save for retirement the way that saving for retirement is advertised.

So your financial advisor says you'll need 70 percent of your income after you stop working. I have a question for you: 70 percent of *what* income? The last year you'll work? No. The year you're having a planning meeting with your advisor. That means that if you're 45, and you sit down with your advisor to figure this out, you will base your retirement plan on the number you make now, rather than the number you could be making when you're 65 years old, or whatever age you decide to slow down. It's complicated enough without factoring in potential raises over the course of a lifetime.

If you are 30 years old and trying to plan the later years of your career, it's unlikely that you are earning an income that is even close to what you will earn in the future. You probably have completely different needs right now and may be saving for a down payment or an engagement ring. You likely have no idea what your life will be like in 30 or 40 years, and you shouldn't feel any pressure to follow these industry standards.

How are you planning for potential increases to your income? Let's say you make $200,000 per year and you're 40 years old. Based on your current trajectory, you will likely make $300,000 by the time you are 50. You happen to like your job and feel confident this scenario will play out. Should you plan to use 70 percent of your current salary for your retirement projection, or 70 percent of $300,000 in 10 years (or $400,000 in 20 years)? If you are like most people in this situation, you aren't afraid to defer some of your current savings in favor of saving for a down payment. I mean, you just had a third kid, and space is tight, so I get it. The problem is that now you are increasing the amount you will need while simultaneously spending a disproportionate amount of your raise on expenses.

As you make more money, it seems like your expenses just keep going up. Are you going to maintain this expense level into retirement? Once you start indulging in fine cuisine at Michelin-starred restaurants, it is unlikely the ribs at Applebee's will hit the same way they once did. This makes it even harder to predict how much money you will have to save toward retirement going forward. Maybe you'll agree to start saving 10 or 15 percent in a few years, but have you thought about how much it will cost to replace your car? And when will you start saving money in a college plan for your kids?

Please don't be discouraged. I want you to improve your lifestyle as you make more money; I also want you to be prepared for a reality where you might have to work longer than what you have been told.

If you think it's hard to predict and plan as someone who works a nine-to-five, the situation is even harder for business owners and entrepreneurs. Most businesses have different financial needs at various times. They need to save and spend money differently, especially in the early stages of their business. Before I ever started maxing out my 401(k) plan, I hired a personal assistant—and I'm in the financial services industry! Before I ever started putting money into a mutual fund, I paid to host wine tasting events for clients and prospective clients. I always knew that I was going to be far more in control of my rate of return by investing in my business than if I put my money into the stock market. Going all the way back to the late 1990s and early 2000s, the stock market did extremely well, and I still did better by investing in my business.

So when I work with entrepreneurs, 9 times out of 10, I tell them *not* to give me their money—they're better off putting it back into their business because they have far more control over the outcome of their work than they do over the outcome of the stock market.

Another assumption the financial industry makes is that you're always going to be able to see the results of your investments on a balance sheet. If you're putting money into your business, you can have a reasonable expectation of the return on the investment, but you won't know for sure until you have a liquidity event or something like it. Until then, it looks like you're investing your money into something with an unpredictable future value.

Throwing Darts

In order to accurately predict how much money you will need to one day retire, you will need to make some additional assumptions.

Will Social Security still be around? Will you be eligible? How much should you plan to receive? As you may recall from chapter 2, Social Security was initially put into place almost a hundred years ago to supplement the income of retired workers who did not live nearly as long after they retired as we do now. Most people are still planning to retire at 65—the same age as workers did in 1940—and Social

Security was not designed to pay a benefit for 30 years. Personally, I am not planning to receive anything—if I do, it will be a nice surprise.

What about inflation? This is an important factor because if someone confidently knows how much they will want to spend in retirement, they need to calculate the future value of that amount. For example, if a 45-year-old thinks they will need $15,000 per month to spend in retirement, that number when they are 65 is roughly $27,000 per month, assuming an inflation of 3 percent. When they are 85, it is almost $50,000. I think 3 percent is a good number to use based on history, although the US (and pretty much every other country) has never carried the amount of debt it currently has. The unprecedented levels of US national debt increase the risk of higher inflation in the long run, which could make retirement spending projections based on historical inflation rates overly optimistic. Retirees will likely need to plan for inflation rates higher than 3 percent if US debt continues rising faster than economic growth.

What tax rates are you assuming in the future? I will share some of my thoughts on tax strategies later in the book, but for now, I want you to understand that your retirement plan would be significantly altered if you were planning on a 30 percent tax rate in retirement and ended up in a 50 percent tax bracket.

Another question I love to ask is, What age will you die? Or how long do you want to live? What about your spouse? The longevity market was valued at $25.1 billion in 2020 and is projected to reach $44.2 billion by 2030.[1] We are finding ways to prolong our lives at a pace that is not slowing down. I typically recommend using the age of 95 for planning purposes, but I worry often that many of us will live well beyond that number. The last thing you want to do is hit age 90 and

Your ability to earn an income is directly correlated with your freedom and the confidence to spend your savings and investments.

realize you are running out of money because you are living much longer than you ever thought possible. The amount of money you will need to retire will change dramatically if you assume that you'll live to age 90 versus 100.

Do you want to leave some money behind as a legacy (for grandchildren or for charitable causes), or do you want to spend down all of your assets? Most people like the idea of leaving some money or assets to their heirs after they pass. Some want to spend every penny. There is no right or wrong answer here. But keep in mind the scary nature of a plan that involves spending your last penny right before you die. This requires predicting exactly how long you will live, which is extremely difficult. If you guess wrong early in retirement and overspend, you may run out of money.

When it comes to predicting the future of Social Security benefits, inflation, tax rates, and when you are going to die, I will forgive you if you feel woefully underqualified to have an opinion. I certainly do, and I have been doing this for over 25 years.

Assumptions They Don't Include

There's one major factor your plan likely doesn't include: How will you react when you stop earning money (if you retire at the traditional age)? What will it feel like not to have an income for what might be the first time in your adult life? How will it feel to spend the money you worked so hard to save?

There is a psychological element to retirement—whether you stop at age 65 or 80—that most people overlook. I have clients who are retired with ample savings, yet only those still earning income spend freely without worry. Ongoing income, whether from work or other sources like royalties or investments, helps clients feel empowered to spend their hard-earned cash. Not to mention the fact that for most of your adult life, you've been watching your bank balances grow year after year, except for a bad year in the market here and there. For the first time, people have to contend with the mental and emotional effects of watching their balances go down because they are now withdrawing more than they are earning.

This uncertainty over spending patterns highlights just how difficult it is to plan for a retirement that feels financially secure. By now you should be able to see how difficult it is to accurately predict so many of the standard inputs that are required to develop a retirement plan. Unfortunately, there are even more factors most advisors don't consider that could deeply impact your finances.

Most people assume they and their significant other are going to be healthy for the rest of their lives. Or they assume their parents will be healthy and won't require their time, effort, or money. Or they assume their parents have been saving responsibly to support themselves in the last years of their lives. At the end of the day, however, who are they going to call when they run out of money? You, and you will undoubtedly begin supporting them. Most people aren't having these conversations with their parents, much less planning to support them.

This is especially true for those facing down a dementia diagnosis in the family. I've often referred to Alzheimer's as the iceberg to your *Titanic*. Your financial plan may appear to be unsinkable until your mother requires 24-7 care to the tune of $5,000 per month that she cannot afford. The reason I use Alzheimer's as an example is because that diagnosis, along with many other forms of dementia, can still leave you or your loved one alive for a very long time. It can bleed you and your family dry because it—and the care it requires—doesn't end quickly.

What about the weddings of your children? Are you factoring in paying for your kids to get married? If you have grandkids, will you add in savings for them, or plan for the money it might take for you to travel to see them?

All of this is to say that your ability to earn an income is directly correlated with your freedom and the confidence to spend your savings and investments.

The point of this chapter isn't to bombard you with questions that are hard to answer; rather, I want you to understand that the few assumptions used to build the typical financial plan aren't remotely enough to get the full picture of your life. I want you to realize that so many of these factors are hard to account and plan for. The answer isn't "just work harder, longer hours." The answer is to change the way you think about retirement.

Hopefully, you're starting to see how building malleability and time into your plan allows you to be flexible when life demands it. Although many of the initial assumptions are a necessary starting point, there is so much more to consider. To keep things simple, I will not be including all the variables you may want to include as we go through the rest of this book and as you build your financial plan. Just keep in mind that whatever metrics you use, the outcome will almost certainly be different 20 years from now, and you'll need to adjust it as you go.

Your Homework

Go check out the calculator at derekcoburn.com/neverretire. When I create a comprehensive financial plan for my clients, the primary goal is to help them better understand how the choices they make might impact them in the future. This tool will help you do the same. Go play with the calculator before you continue reading this book, and make sure to start with the assumption that you'll retire at 65. There is an overview on the website to ensure you understand how to use the calculator successfully.

The calculator is pre-populated with some assumptions that you can adjust. You can enter your current age and the age when you want to retire, as well as your current income and savings. Just like in our "Tale of Two Tonys," you will be able to see how much more you need to save based on how long you work.

Plug in the amount of money you think you'll want to live on when you stop working (which will be a percentage of your current income). Don't worry about being super accurate right now—we already know it's difficult to predict what you'll want in the future. Just ballpark it.

The calculator will reveal whether you are on track, and if not, how much you need to save each month in order to make it happen.

Next, try entering 75 as the age of retirement instead of 65. What happens? How does that change what you need to save? How does that change your trajectory for maintaining funds, or running out of them? Most people find that their outlook changes drastically with the addition of even 5 years, not to mention 10 years.

I have also added a field for you to enter income after retirement. Essentially, you could explore a scenario where you "retire" from your current work at age 55 and then assume an income stream from a different source for 15 to 20 years.

This is an exercise you can revisit frequently to help you feel better about the decisions you make around money in real time. If you understand how working longer changes your horizon, it puts you in a stronger position to make better decisions on saving for your children's education, transitioning to a new career, or buying a second home. The point here is to ease your mind about where you stand financially, and to help you begin to create a stronger, more realistic financial plan for yourself.

{ 5 }

Your Many Options

B Y NOW, I hope you've begun to embrace the idea that traditional retirement is not only not feasible but not even desirable. In this chapter, I want to invite you to fully let the idea of traditional retirement go, and instead focus on how you might arrange your working life in a way that brings more meaning and fulfillment so you won't want to stop working. Once you acknowledge that you'll be working for an additional 20 or 30 years, you can explore more flexible arrangements in work and life. Instead of putting off important relationships, your health, or your sense of play in the name of work, you can combine them and enjoy life to the fullest—now and later.

As entrepreneur and author Alex Hormozi noted, we're made to work:

> In the Bible, before God gave Adam a wife, he gave him a job. We're made to work. For all of human history except for the last 75 years, we have worked until we die. Retirement is a new concept that's fooled the masses. The goals we achieve die with us. Meaning the work we do, not [what] we achieve from it, is the only goal that really mattered to

begin with. *Work isn't the way to achieve the goal. It is the goal.*[1] [emphasis added]

Ideally, your work is not just a means to an end or a way to get more money. Your work should be fulfilling and lucrative in a way that supports your lifestyle. At a minimum, your work should provide you with the resources to shine in other areas of your life. In the following pages, we'll explore approaches to your work life that create opportunities for greater enjoyment in the present, while ensuring you can continue doing work you love in the future.

Transition to a New Career

Transitioning to a new career might be appealing for a variety of reasons. Maybe you hate your work, employer, or clients. Maybe you like, but don't love, any of them. Maybe, like many of my attorney clients, you know you will burn out if you continually bill 2,500 hours per year. Maybe you feel lukewarm about your current situation. Talent and passion don't necessarily go hand in hand, as my friend Philip McKernan would say, so if you've been duking it out in a job that you're good at but don't have a passion for anymore, transitioning might be the best option for you.

This is where most people land—they can't imagine working beyond 65 because they don't want to keep doing what they are doing now for the rest of their lives. I firmly believe it's not work that's the problem; it's the kind of work they're doing. They stay in miserable jobs because of their financial goals, or because they have a certain lifestyle they or their families don't want to give up. Or they stay because what they want to do feels completely out of reach or daunting to pursue. In the process, they shortcut the potential for fulfillment.

Faryn Clark and her husband were living what most would consider a successful life—she worked in corporate America, and he had a successful career in oil and gas. Both were at the height of their careers, but they were starting to question the cost. Her company constantly moved their family around the US, which became exhausting, and it dawned on her that her life was not her own if her employer could tell her to pick up and move at the drop of a hat. While her husband was successful, he started to question what he was doing, and what life was all about. They had some money but not much fulfillment.

They were living in Dallas, Texas, when Faryn was told she would have to move to Cincinnati if she wanted to be promoted, and that's when she drew the line. She quit to open her own skincare spa. It felt like a new peak until she realized that the culture she had settled into was extremely competitive—there was a right neighborhood to live in, the right house to own, and the right school for her children to attend. They had changed environments, but they still felt stuck in the rat race.

Faryn and her husband started to wonder, *What would it look like if we were actually passionate about what we did? What would it look like if we never had to retire because we loved our work so much?* They started to think about what they wanted for their kids too. At the time, their three children were still young, all under the age of ten. They wanted their children to have a global perspective, and they wanted to volunteer and help others while traveling.

At some point during this period of soul searching, Faryn and her family were on vacation in Cabo San Lucas, Mexico. She had always been in love with Mexico and had traveled there often. Faryn and her husband were sitting on the beach on Thanksgiving Day when she suggested they sell everything and move to Mexico. It wasn't the first time she had suggested this to her husband. He said, "There's no way you can run your business from Mexico. You're crazy." She said, "I want to pray about it. I want to put it out there." So she did.

In January, late on a Friday afternoon, Faryn got a call out of the blue from a local broker she had been talking to—someone wanted to buy her business. She instinctively replied that it wasn't for sale. She doubted anyone was going to pay her what it was worth, since it was the top franchise in the country. He told her to think about it over the weekend and he would call her the following Monday. "Just give me a number," he said. When he called again, she gave him the number. He said, "Great, can you close in two weeks?" She couldn't believe her luck. Here was the chance to unplug, let everything go, and start fresh. "Everything throughout my last ten years has unfolded in a way where I happened to be at the right place at the right time. When you're in alignment, everything falls into place," she says.

Soon after the sale, she and her family sold everything and "pulled the plug." Everyone thought they were crazy, but they were sure they had to make a dramatic change to be able to connect with their passion and purpose.

They had zero plans when they arrived in Mexico. They knew what they loved to do, and they wanted to dive deeper into the things that brought them joy. Faryn had an interest in philanthropy but didn't know how that would apply to her life at first. Through researching and learning about her options, she realized she could support people who were amazingly talented but didn't have the same fortunate circumstances she did.

Faryn started out by connecting with Mexican artisans whose work she loved, exploring ways to help them through options such as microloans or other opportunities they wouldn't otherwise have. Her work slowly evolved into a profitable business with a massive social impact. She partnered with local artists and created a business to help them share their gifts with more people around the world. Faryn feels like she is living out her purpose and does not plan to ever retire from this work.

Don't wait any longer to pursue what interests you. If you feel like you're treading water or just working for the money, I encourage you to come up with a plan, or at least take the first steps toward a more enjoyable professional experience. Test the waters and determine if there is a market for the skill you have or want to develop. Is there a way you can begin to work in this field, even if you're still working full-time? Actively transitioning out of your current job could help you move forward with your life and find meaning right now.

If you feel the need to stay in your current role until you are 65 to be financially independent, transitioning to a career that you will happily continue into your 70s or 80s—even if you earn much less than you do now—will allow you to leave your current situation much earlier than you were planning. More income each year beyond 65 equals less money you need to pull from investments, which means you won't need to save as much right now as you think.

Build a Side Business

We've all heard about the idea of creating income on the side, such as driving for Uber or DoorDash, or managing Airbnb properties. While those are great options (and I could imagine myself driving around, listening to music, and delivering food to people), I think there's also an opportunity to come up with creative ideas of your own making—ones that fulfill some deep need that your current work doesn't and may take you somewhere new.

Ideas are everywhere. For example, there are a lot of opportunities to work with older people. I'm half-joking as I write this, but what about the idea of "rent a granddad"? We know that older folks, especially those who live in retirement homes, really need interaction and struggle with loneliness, and they tend to feel isolated from the rest of the world. What if you were to set up a business where you paired an older person with young kids so they could share stories, do puzzles, and impart wisdom (supervised, of course)? Everyone benefits from an arrangement like that. You could also consider creating services for seniors who need help paying bills, dealing with technology, or getting to and from appointments.

I have a passion for music, and seeing live music always inspires a flow state in me. I never understand it when people tell me they don't like it, and I'm convinced it's because they're listening to the wrong music. I have this fantasy of doing for music what Jay Baer is doing for tequila. Jay Baer is a world-class speaker and prolific author; he also had a full life and career as the owner of a marketing agency. To create more time and a slower pace for himself, he sold the agency in the middle of the COVID pandemic. He also created some videos as a hobby around one of his favorite passions: tequila.

Initially, this involved opening TikTok and Instagram accounts, where he shared his reviews of tequila brands and all things tequila-related in an effort to make his favorite liquor accessible to more people. This idea had been stewing for some time. Fifteen years prior, Jay had a conversation with entrepreneur Gary Vaynerchuk about creating content around tequila, similar to how Vaynerchuk created content around wine. At the time, Jay was too busy running the agency and raising

Ideally, your work is not just a means to an end or a way to get more money.

two young kids, so he didn't pursue the idea. Now, with all this newfound time on his hands, he had the space to think more creatively and build something that was more in line with one of his passions.

Jay started by making videos about tequila and sharing them daily to grow a following. Over time, the tequila content channel grew into a lucrative business, generating mid-six-figure revenue as an influencer gig. He was able to leverage his expertise and relationships in the tequila industry to build a consulting business for tequila brands as well. He jokes that more people recognize him in the airport for his tequila business than they do as a professional speaker.

Your passions will be different. The point is that there are a lot of great ways to earn money on the side, whether you want to build a small business that depends on you and your schedule or build a business that can expand and grow.

When I started out, I grew my wealth management practice to the point where I was doing well enough to qualify to go on trips with the top financial advisors in my company around the world. I was always at least 10 years younger than everyone else on these trips. It made me curious about what life would look like if I continued down this path, working hard in this industry. With every trip I took, I spoke to the financial advisors about their businesses and how they had built them. Almost all of them had between 1,500 and 2,000 clients at the time, but they only seemed to really enjoy working with about 20 percent of them. In the financial services business, we're much more limited in terms of how we can attract new clients. We can't do a lot of social media marketing and even word of mouth is problematic. It almost seems like the prevailing business strategy is to wait for clients to fall into your lap. Because of that, if a client refers you to their family or friends, the typical financial advisor will happily work with them, even if they aren't a great fit personality-wise or business-wise.

When my wife, Melanie, got pregnant with our first child, I was working 60 to 70 hours per week, and while the business was going well, I was spending most of my time with people I didn't love, which made the work I loved much less enjoyable. Once she had our son, I wanted to be available to spend more time with my family. This really motivated me to make some changes to my business and my lifestyle so I could live a more balanced life. I had about 350 clients, and as with my mentors, I could honestly say I truly enjoyed working with only 20 percent of them. The other 80 percent had personality quirks I didn't like, or investing philosophies that didn't jibe, or didn't listen to my advice. Already I was clear that I didn't want to go down the path of accumulating thousands of clients and nurturing mediocre relationships. At the same time, I was learning about social media marketing but couldn't use any of it in my industry, which frustrated me. Even now, I can't even have my wealth management information on my LinkedIn profile for compliance reasons if I want to also include my other endeavors—it's that ridiculous.

I had grown my existing wealth management practice by hosting smaller un-networking events, wine tastings, and roundtable lunches. As I mentioned in my previous book, *Networking Is Not Working*, these helped me grow my business with a focus on quality over quantity. They also gave me a good feel for what worked when helping people form connections and what didn't, to the point where I thought I could turn it into a side business.

At the time, I was working long hours and had a newborn. I really didn't have time to start another business. To do it, I would have to free up some of my time... which led me to cut 80 percent of my wealth management clients to launch a new business with Melanie, CADRE, which we still run today. After the cut, my wealth management business had only 75 clients, which made it so much more enjoyable because I loved working with and growing with them. And it gave me the time to fill CADRE with people my wife and I absolutely loved.

Today, CADRE has over 125 curated members from across North America, and we offer unique opportunities for business growth, personal development, and connection for CEOs and entrepreneurs. With both virtual and online events, we focus on facilitating significant breakthroughs in the lives and businesses of our already successful members by providing access to exceptional people and ideas. CADRE takes a lot of time and effort to maintain, but it doesn't feel that way because we both love it so much.

Launching a side business felt a little scary at first, but in the end, I didn't take much of a pay cut because of the 80-20 Rule: I kept the 20 percent of my clients who generated 80 percent of my income. There were clients I chose to cut even though they generated good revenue, but for the most part I ended my work with those who didn't match my values or have the asset levels to make it worth my while.

One of the main tenets of CADRE is that members show up focused on how they can add value for other people, as opposed to focused on how they can get value. People have asked how Melanie and I brought together such an amazing group of people, and for a long time, I didn't have a good answer to that question. After a while, it dawned on me that one of the most important ancillary benefits of having two streams of income at the same time was the flexibility to really stick to my guns in terms of who was an ideal fit for each business and who wasn't—something I may not have had the courage to do if I only relied on one business. If I identified someone who may have come to CADRE with selfish motives, it was easy to say no to their monthly membership fee because I didn't need that money to pay my mortgage. Through cutting the majority of my practice—something that looked crazy on paper—I made as much money (and eventually more) as I had before. More importantly, the move made me happier because it gave me the chance to spend time working exclusively with people I loved.

There may come a day when I let go of one or both of those businesses, but running two businesses at the same time has allowed me to do work that keeps me fulfilled, to provide well for my family, and to live the life I want now. If you don't feel ready to give up your current career but have interests that extend beyond it, this is an excellent way to have both.

Transition to Consulting or Coaching

Tom Graham retired from the Potomac Electric Power Company (Pepco), which supplies electric power to the city of Washington, DC, and surrounding communities in Maryland, after 30 years. When he was growing up, his father taught him that the best way to succeed was to get a job with the government or a utility company, work 30 years, and get a pension. He started off in an entry-level marketing position and went on to hold several leadership positions that included president of the entire region.

After he announced his retirement, his colleagues asked him to reconsider, and to think about staying and working in a different capacity. As accomplished as he was, he also really looked forward to traditional retirement. Up until that point, all he could focus on was his final date: June 16, 2016. By that time his financials goals were met, and his professional goals had been exceeded. However, he began to see that his journey wasn't finished. Most of what he had known was work, and he knew life would be uncomfortable and empty without it. He says the Monday after he retired was one of the hardest days of his life, and he believes this is likely the case for many others.

After a very brief stint doing nothing, Tom elected to join a number of boards in diverse industries, which gave him the chance to make a meaningful contribution, but they generally met only quarterly. Even more exciting, Tom's deep experience in his field led him to several opportunities, leading to him creating his own consultancy business. His first client was his former employer. The relationships he maintained running his consultancy business led him to the opportunity to chair a board that built an $18 million multisport complex in his community that serves thousands of youths and adults.

With his consultancy business, all the relationships Tom built over his long career can still benefit both him and his colleagues. He gets to pick and choose his clients, all of whom are people he's worked with before on projects that are personally meaningful. The trust he had with his employer and colleagues took years to build, and he still gets to capitalize on it. He doesn't market or have employees or financial targets, because he doesn't need to—three decades of hard work built those contacts and trust in spades. He didn't have to learn an entirely new skillset, and he set up his consulting business on his own terms. And Tom periodically takes breaks to travel or spend time with his kids.

Tom views his version of retirement as liberating because it gives him time with his family, time to travel and play golf, and a way to do community service work on his own terms. He enjoys business as usual but is not wedded to it. Now he focuses on how he will make a difference today.

Starting a consulting business makes a lot of sense if you've accrued years of experience and relationships within an industry. If you've got a strong reputation, your wide network still has a lot of respect for you and the work you've done—and they'll likely be interested in hiring you for your wisdom and connections. Consulting tends to pay fairly well and lends itself to building a lifestyle with a lot of flexibility and control over hours worked and level of involvement.

A coaching business is also an option. While consulting tends to focus on strategy and solutions for specific problems, coaching zeroes in on personal development and long-term growth. There is significant overlap between the two, however. Both work toward helping those struggling along the path behind us. As entrepreneur Ed Mylett said, "You're most qualified to help the person you used to be,"[2] emphasizing the idea that you can draw from your experiences to guide and support people who are now striving to achieve what you have already accomplished.

Take a Sabbatical or Mini-Retirement

A sabbatical and a mini-retirement both involve taking an extended break from work, but they differ in purpose, duration, and how they are perceived, both personally and professionally.

Let's talk about sabbaticals first. A sabbatical is a practice that comes from academia and allows professors to take a certain time off (such as a semester or a year) to focus on their research, studies, or professional development. The concept has been adopted by other industries, with many of the same ideas: they provide time off for further education, rejuvenation, or learning something new and useful in your job. Sabbaticals usually last a few months to a year, and they're supported by the employer because the employee will eventually return to work. In a lot of cases, the position is held open for the employee. Employers might fully or partially pay employees during their time off, although they may also opt not to pay them at all.

I had a client named Tina who, about 10 years ago, had an epiphany around the idea of sabbaticals. She was a partner at a major law firm—successful, earning seven figures every year. We sat down to do her annual review, and she mentioned that while her work was going great and she was making good money, she felt like she was missing the best years of her three children's lives.

It obviously bothered her very much, and I asked her if she felt like she could continue working beyond 60 or 65 years of age. She said, "Absolutely, as long as my firm or some other firm will have me. I would love to be doing this into my old age." Since that was the case, I suggested she take a few years off.

As with the average person expecting to retire in their 60s, her immediate fear was that it wouldn't work financially. But when we plugged in the numbers, creating a retirement age of 70 instead of 60 or 65, they lined up perfectly. She could take a sabbatical without hurting herself financially.

She stepped aside for three years and was able to spend more time with her family, knowing that it wouldn't negatively affect her retirement or her family's financials down the road because she would make up for lost time by doing what she loved anyway, after her kids were fully grown and out of the nest.

Now, it goes without saying that my client was in good standing with her firm. They were more than happy to give her the time off and have her back when she was ready to return—in no small part because of her skill as a lawyer. She not only loved her job but also was very good at it, and there was no question that her colleagues wanted her to return.

I stress this because I want to be sure that you don't run out and quit tomorrow under the impression that you can show up 12 months later and ask for your job back. That's why sabbaticals are a little bit easier for those who work in an industry where you can take that kind of time off. They work best if you're well established in your career and have a solid relationship with your employer.

Mini-retirements, on the other hand, involve taking an extended break from your career. The idea was popularized by Tim Ferriss in his book *The 4-Hour Workweek*, as a way to enjoy the benefits of retirement at different stages in life. Like sabbaticals, these can vary greatly and range from a few months to years. The difference is that these are often open-ended and not usually supported or formalized by employers because they are seen as a personal choice, unrelated to professional development. Taking a mini-retirement might involve quitting a job or taking leave without a formal expectation that you return to the same position, or to the company at all. Mini-retirements are also more often self-funded.

And they don't have to be a drain on your savings. Ferriss believes that mini-retirements can improve your financial life. Most people assume they will spend money during a mini-retirement, so they need to save up for it or pull from their retirement accounts to fund the break. Ferriss doesn't believe that's always the case. For example, he traveled as he took his mini-retirement, forgoing the expenses on his expensive apartment in San Francisco by subletting it, as well as all of the transportation costs associated with living there. This resulted in a savings of $32,000 for him. His point is mini-retirements are not by definition a drag on finances.[3]

A friend of mine, Ati Williams, opted for a mini-retirement at just 40 years of age. She and her then-husband worked at a real estate brokerage and also owned and ran a development company called Honeycomb. Their primary work was to flip homes, specifically condo conversions. Once in a while they had institutional personal investors, but for the most part they funded all of it. She used to call her business the "second shift," because she would work her day job until 4 p.m., spend time with her daughter, and after her daughter went to bed, she would work again from 7 p.m. till late.

By the time she took her mini-retirement, Ati had been on overdrive for too long. She felt it had to be all or nothing: there was no way to ease off that kind of schedule and lifestyle. She knew herself well enough to know that she would have to go cold turkey to get the break she really needed. So she and her husband hired someone to take care of their Washington, DC-based business for them and moved to the West Coast.

During her one-year mini-retirement, Ati led a simpler life and enjoyed doing things like going to the supermarket, reading the newspaper in the morning, and taking a few much-needed vacations. She also spent time thinking about what she wanted to do, who she wanted to work with, and how many clients she wanted to have at a time. She reviewed the last stretch of her career, and the new space allowed her to see her strengths and weaknesses more clearly.

Ati completely restructured her business based on her reflections. She decided she only wanted to work with people who live close by; most of her clients now live in her neighborhood, which makes it easy for her to get to the site, saving time commuting and making meetings better because they're often in person. She also changed the starting rate of the projects she works on, from $200,000 remodels to larger, more expensive projects that range from $400,000 to $600,000. This makes it easy for her to have fewer projects at a time.

After moving to California, Ati became a licensed general contractor, which made her eligible to try out for *Hack My Home*, a popular Netflix show where she and four other designers come up with innovative ways to transform family homes. She hadn't planned on becoming the host of a show, but it all happened because she reapproached her business. Now she does a lot of speaking at home-and-garden shows and in entrepreneur circles, particularly on what it's like to be a woman in a male-dominated industry.

Ati's financial process doesn't follow the standard plan. "My advisor's biggest complaint is that I'm not diverse enough," she jokes. Although she does have some stock investments, she says real estate is in her blood and her primary form of investing. She knows she can get a better return, so she plans to liquidate some of her assets when it's time to take her next mini-retirement and pay for college, which she plans to take when her daughter graduates from high school. She's seen enough parents become empty-nesters and lose their minds, so she plans on packing in a whole lot of fun trips with her daughter in the year before and sporadic visits to her daughter's school once she's settled in. "My daughter is so awesome; I would hang out with her even if she wasn't my kid," she says.

Ati doesn't plan to stop working at all, but she does plan to change the way she works. She wants to build in more space and time in her schedule. She might decide to work fewer days in a week. At the same time, she knows she gets fired up by results, and if she didn't work, she'd "shrivel up and die." She looks forward to potentially mentoring other business owners and speaking in the future.

When people save aggressively for retirement, they often put off the fun, extravagant trips they want to experience. We've talked so far about mini-retirements in the context of taking more time off, but you can also consider taking a short

If you've still got wisdom to share and you love your career, you can set up your work time on your terms.

time to indulge in an experience that you dreamed would be part of your later years. For example, Melanie and I took a two-week trip to Europe, where we saw Taylor Swift perform in Amsterdam and Pearl Jam perform twice in Barcelona, and dined at five Michelin-starred restaurants. It was a great time. It took a lot of planning, money, and effort to execute, but I came back a better, well-rested, happier, and more emotionally available father, friend, and professional because of the time I took to have some fun with my wife. Consider the idea that part of your commitment to having mini-retirements could include enjoying the fruits of your labor more now, instead of waiting until later.

In essence, the concept of a mini-retirement is to take the block of 25 years you might have had in your traditional retirement and break it up over the course of your life. This will give you space to step back and evaluate, to play and enjoy life, and to potentially pivot into a new career if it suits you to do so.

Pursue Your Life's Calling

While rare (for now), several people have already found their calling, and if they have it their way, they will do it until they drop dead. Even though they are confident they will "work" for a long time, most of these folks in my experience are still planning for a traditional retirement. They want to be financially independent so they won't be required to work—they want to work because they want to, not because they have to. These folks are also more likely to worry about what will happen if they become unhealthy or disabled, so they justify heroic savings efforts as a "just in case" measure. I don't know about you, but if I become disabled in my 70s after working and saving hard my whole life while forgoing more time with family and friends, traveling, and so on, I won't look back and say, "Thank God I worked and saved so hard all those years!"

Michael Gottlieb, my attorney and founder of Momentum Law Group, is fortunate to be one of those folks who loves what they do. He's also fortunate to have realized this early on. Not long into his career as a lawyer, all anyone could talk about was the massive lottery payout; everyone around Michael kept asking what he would do if he won the lottery. He didn't play the lottery, so he didn't really think about it that much, but the question made him wonder what he would do. It dawned on him that he would take a two-week vacation because, at that time, he'd never done so. Then he'd come right back home and continue doing the work he was meant to do. It was refreshing to realize that he loved his work and would continue doing it no matter how much money he had.

Michael did have a moment of doubt: during COVID, he considered retiring, even though he was only in his forties. "Everything was dark, and it absolutely sucked," he says. His work stopped being fun, and he missed the day-to-day interactions with his colleagues and clients. It was hard for him to see everyone around him so sad. During a discussion with his wife, Sue, he told her that he was considering retiring. Although they could make it work, they would have to change their lifestyle. Sue asked him to wait it out; she knew that Michael liked working with people, and COVID made it hard to do that. She encouraged him to see what happened on the other side of the pandemic, to see if he still felt the same way. By the time the pandemic was coming to a resolution, Michael was back to working with colleagues and had realized how much he loved being a lawyer—it was never the work, it was working remotely that he hated.

That experience helped him realize that he loved his work too much to retire. He decided to continue working into his later years, with the intention of slowing down at some point. This would allow his family to live a very generous lifestyle into the future without thinking about how that might have to change. It also allowed them to have experiences they might otherwise put off. Michael and Sue finally got to take their two-week vacation with their kids; they went to Italy and explored all over the country, including a full-day private tour of the Lamborghini and Pagani museums. He was even a little mad that it took them so long to get to the place where they could do that. The experience was so incredible that Michael decided he wanted to take those kinds of trips more often, and working later in life will help support that decision.

Michael now loves being in a position where they don't have to worry about being frugal and saving hard. The reason it took him so long to have a wonderful two-week vacation with his family was because he was working and saving aggressively for a traditional retirement. It felt too indulgent to spend that kind of money on a frivolous holiday. But now that he's accepted he will work longer, he has all kinds of plans to take trips with his family that will create lasting memories.

Michael's decision to keep working also makes it easier to spend time with his kids. His daughter is now in college, and when she went through a tough adjustment phase, he was ready to get on a plane and book a hotel without a second thought because they knew they could afford to take a relaxed approach to visits. He's taken several long-weekend trips with his daughter to New York, Chicago, and Toronto. His son is growing up, and Michael knows he doesn't have much time left with him at home. For his graduation, his son asked to go on a car rally together. It's an expensive but life-changing four- or five-day adventure. For Michael, it's a win-win: he gets to spend time with his son and have an incredible experience.

If you get to wake up every day and do the thing you love, are you investing some of your time and money into your relationships and well-being to ensure you'll be able to do your work forever? If you take better care of yourself, it is far more likely that you will live a long life and be able to better serve your clients along the way. Most of us know this, but adhering to typical retirement planning advice seems to take precedence over a more practical approach.

Plan to Slow Down or Pivot

Also among the lucky who currently feel they are doing the work they were put on this planet to do are folks who would like to eventually slow down at some point. Even though they love what they do, they don't want to do it for over 40 hours every week for the rest of their lives. If you can relate, my question for you is, Why wait until retirement?

Instead of grinding away at 40 hours per week for 20 years and then cutting back to 20 hours per week for 20 years, why not explore an arrangement where you work 30 hours per week indefinitely? This is just one of many examples you could experiment with. Earlier in the book, I asked you to consider whether your children would rather spend time with you when they're 10 or when they're 40, or whether your spouse would prefer monthly dates and multiple getaways a year now or romance later in life. Those are years you don't get back.

John had been in the real estate business for over three decades and his work was not just a job but a part of his identity. He loved the thrill of closing a deal, the satisfaction of helping people find their dream home, and the ever-changing dynamics of the property market. As he got closer to his 60s, he began to feel the toll of the long hours and constant availability. He wanted to build a life where he could claim time for himself so he could spend it with his friends and family. But he didn't want to give up the work he loved.

Instead of retiring, John decided to scale back gradually over five years. He transitioned from working 50-to-60-hour weeks to a more manageable 25 hours a week. This shift allowed him to maintain his professional identity and keep his business thriving, while also achieving a healthier work-life balance. By that point in his career, he had amassed a very large network of clients, and his reduced hours allowed him to be selective about which of them he chose to work with.

He didn't just jump into this transition though. He started identifying the most critical aspects of his work that required his direct involvement—and that he loved the most. He focused on high-impact activities, such as client meetings, negotiations, and strategic planning.

Over the years, John had built a trusted team. By delegating more operational tasks and routine client interactions to his most capable colleagues, he made sure that the quality of service remained high without his constant presence. He also adopted a schedule that allowed him to work during the most productive hours of the day, so he had time in the afternoon to do whatever he wished.

The change in pace brought a lot of benefits—John got to slow down but keep his working relationships and his fulfilling job. He was more energized than ever, especially when he realized that the cut to his earnings was not as deep as he had feared, because he was now able to serve the most lucrative clients without distraction. He got to travel with his family and took a few trips with friends too. And he finally got to experience life without being available 24-7.

If you love your work but seek a better balance, scaling back hours while maintaining meaningful involvement can be a rewarding path. Slowing down doesn't have to be drastic: you don't have to launch a total overhaul of your career or go part-time right away. I've got a lot of clients and friends who decided to change their work and the time they spend on it by adjusting their working schedules. You could vow to never work on Fridays. You could decide that you'll take a long, four-day weekend once a month, or take one month off every summer so you can spend it with your kids or take a vacation with friends. You could change your hours so you only work during the times of day that suit you best.

If you've still got wisdom to share and you love your career, you can set up your work time on your terms. You wouldn't be alone in doing this either. A 2024 study from the life insurance company Allianz Life showed that 47 percent of Americans see themselves gradually shifting away from work, as opposed to stopping cold turkey.[4] Baby Boomers lead the shift in this thinking: 58 percent think about retirement as a gradual transition, while 53 percent of Gen Xers and 45 percent of Millennials feel the same.[5] Planning on an income stream from 65 on will open up a lot of flexibility for you right now, even if the income stream is smaller than what you are earning now.

There are a lot of ways to rethink how you work. Related to slowing down and taking control of your schedule is the idea of pivoting how you work. In Stephen Cope's perennial seller, *The Great Work of Your Life,* he shares a story about a pastor who came from a long line of spiritual leaders. His lineage influenced his decision to become a pastor, but he was deeply unhappy with the work and felt like he had chosen the wrong path. Through a lot of deep personal exploration, the pastor realized that he was inspired and moved by the work of composing and playing organ music. He was literally in the right building; he was just in the wrong role.

If you're not happy in your career, start looking at your skills and how you might use them in a way that helps you build the life you want. One licensed therapist, whom we'll call Mary, didn't like her industry's reliance on specific diagnoses and the restrictive, often medication-based ways of treating clients. For a while, she thought about quitting altogether. Then she realized that she could take what she loved about therapy—talking with people and helping them through their problems—and build a coaching practice, allowing her to bring her vast experience to the field but forgo the need to deal with diagnoses and insurance companies. This also helped her refine whom she wanted to work with, since her favorite clients were entrepreneurs and self-starters—people who were highly likely to hire a coach for personal development. She didn't need to throw the baby out with the bathwater. She just had to take a fresh look at how she could use her skills and create the sandbox she wanted to play in.

There are probably a lot of folks out there right now who feel like they're in the wrong place, while in reality, they just need to make small changes to the way they work. Think about ways you can strip away the parts of your work that you don't enjoy, so you can do the things that create happiness and fulfillment for you—and the people you work with. You're probably not as far from a fulfilling career as you think you are.

Your Homework

I hope you are starting to see how traditional retirement advice doesn't apply to everyone, because not everyone wants a traditional retirement. There are plenty of additional options to consider.

Whether you decide to take a sabbatical or a longer mini-retirement, or even if you don't have the flexibility to do either of those things at this moment, you need to create some space in your life to explore a change. The people in this chapter share the experience of having taken time away from their work, and that space is what allowed the best next option to emerge. We need to break free of the routines in our lives and give ourselves the gift of a slightly less distracted mind to explore the full range of what is possible for us. You can start by freeing up one hour per week to explore other potential interests or industries to see what you like or don't like. You might have to do this at night when everyone else is asleep, or take a Saturday or Sunday morning to do your research, but it's important that you set aside this time to explore all the possibilities.

All of us waste time somewhere, whether it's watching an hour or two of Netflix, playing video games, or scrolling through Facebook. Sure, you need some time to unplug, but see if you can use some of that downtime to start exploring the things that interest you, learn something new, or revisit an old hobby or passion. Always liked Shakespeare? Volunteer at the local Bard summer festival and see some shows up close. It might spark something.

Consider how flexibility in the timing of your breaks, or in the timing of your workdays, might affect your plan. I know people who take off summers. I know people who take off Fridays. If you build a business, you will have a lot of control over the way you design your day. You could decide that you'll only work in the morning, or that you'll create a midweek break and take every Wednesday afternoon off so you can have lunch with your spouse or a friend. You can sacrifice a little bit of short-term revenue in the name of the type of lifestyle that is most ideal and best suited for you. Also consider the timing of your sabbaticals—for example, you could plan to take a year off when your child graduates high school. Knowing this 5 or 10 years in advance will allow you to craft your life and your financial plan to serve that sabbatical.

Also, every one of these ideas may require that you think about how you might need to cut back on your spending or reduce your lifestyle to support your plans. In the short term, it might feel like you're taking two steps backward. That's all right—it's only temporary, and you'll ultimately be in a better position once the transition is completed. It also helps if you have some cash in the bank. Making these hard choices now will give you the short-term flexibility to step away and create a better life for yourself.

So, after you decide to take a sabbatical or a mini-retirement, or transition into a new job entirely, what's next? That's what we'll cover in the next chapter.

{ 6 }

The Changing World of Work

WHETHER WE like it or not, our jobs and workplaces will be changing drastically over the next few decades due to artificial intelligence (AI) and automation. I don't share this to scare you—instead, I'm trying to get you to grasp the reality of the situation we're all in. Goldman Sachs estimated that "roughly two-thirds of current jobs are exposed to some degree of AI automation and that generative AI could substitute up to one-fourth of current work."[1] McKinsey Global Institute also estimated that 29.5 percent of all hours worked face potential automation by 2030.[2]

According to McKinsey, jobs of the future will focus more on tasks that can't be replaced by machines, such as communicating with people, managing staff, and applying high-level expertise. Jobs that require predictable physical labor, or data processing or collecting—anything repetitive—are the most likely to be replaced by AI.[3] So, if this is the work you do, it will likely change or no longer exist in 10 years. In fact, our brains are already obsolete compared to much of the tech that's available to handle these things. However, AI cannot replace creative thinking, emotional cognizance, and specific kinds of problem-solving that the human brain excels at.

So what does that mean for you? Two things: First, the job you're in now is almost certainly going to change. Second, new jobs will be created and available for you in 10 years that aren't even on our radar now.

Before you get overly concerned about your job going away, let me share some good news. It is very likely that you will be able to earn an income with a lot more flexibility in the future. Want to work 10 hours per week? Want to work only four months each year? Want to do all of this work in your pajamas between 6 p.m. and 11 p.m.? No problem! Any or all of these options are available now and will very likely become close to normal over the next decade. Of course, the more value you can deliver, the more options you'll have.

Already, the number of freelancers has increased drastically. A 2023 Upwork study found that 64 million Americans performed freelance work that year, an all-time high, representing 38 percent of the entire US workforce, and an increase of 4 million total professionals from 2022.[4] The study also showed that 8.3 million professionals, or 13 percent of all US freelancers, were aged 59 or above.[5] It used to be that freelancing was a second choice endeavor, one taken on after a layoff or some other circumstance that forced workers out of a traditional nine-to-five job. Now it seems as though freelancing will serve as the ideal outcome for anyone looking to work on their own terms.

Even more encouraging, the rate of entrepreneurialism in seniors is growing too. Data from the 2019 UPS Store Inside Small Business Survey revealed that 65 percent of Americans dream of opening a small business.[6] The survey also found

You already have a lot of the skills that will be needed in the future, and the jobs that will be available haven't even been invented yet.

that 54 percent say they would rather open a small business than retire, if money or health were not a factor later in life.[7] What's more, a 2008 study at Northwestern University concluded that "a 55-year-old and even a 65-year-old have significantly more innovation potential than a 25-year-old."[8] It turns out that entrepreneurship is not just a game for the young after all.

No matter how the workforce changes or how technology evolves, it will be difficult (if not impossible) to replace those traits that are innate to human expression. From the World Economic Forum's 2023 *Future of Jobs Report*[9] comes this list of "human skills" that will be needed in years to come:

1. Analytical thinking
2. Creative thinking
3. Resilience, flexibility, and agility
4. Motivation and self-awareness
5. Curiosity and lifelong learning
6. Technological literacy
7. Dependability and attention to detail
8. Empathy and active listening
9. Leadership and social influence
10. Quality control

In short, jobs that require judgment and decision-making, nuanced and complex communication skills, creativity and the ability to innovate, and emotional intelligence will not easily be replaced by AI.

You already have a lot of the skills that will be needed in the future, and the jobs that will be available haven't even been invented yet. Instead of feeling fear, look at the future with optimism—there are so many opportunities available.

Skills and Training

Maybe you're worried that you won't have the skills or training to do anything else. This is a common fear, given that a lot of us are working in jobs right now that will not exist in another 20 years. I'm not suggesting anyone quit their job or sell their business tomorrow to avoid slowly fading into irrelevance. What I do suggest is that you start to think about the other skills or passions you have. Think about what excites you. What do you see yourself doing? What have you always wanted to do? What did you love doing when you were a kid? What have you been curious about lately? Think about the hobbies you have now and how you like to spend your free time and be open to the possibility that there might be ways you can turn those passions into a business. Remember, Jay Baer is making more money than most of us by drinking tequila and talking about it on video. And I believe that you, too, have a gift that needs to be shared with the world!

If you're a Millennial, you already understand that you won't be working in the same job or career for the rest of your life. Millennials will typically hold 11 different jobs before they reach their 45th birthday. Interestingly, Millennials also find meaning and purpose in a job to be more important than monetary compensation or benefits. Granted, they are also less likely to own a home and may choose not to own a car. They have less overhead, but they do have more skills and may end up with a more flexible work arrangement, forgoing the 40 hours a week for 20 or 30 hours a week. This only propagates the freelance market, which, as we've said, is growing fast.

What that means is that whether you want to start your own business or work as a freelancer or part-time worker, there will be a lot of companies that are increasingly flexible about their work arrangements. Older workers especially will have a lot of wisdom and experience to contribute, and could do so for just 10 to 20 hours per week, or for a few months out of every year. The point is you can do the work you want to do on your terms.

In his book *Wisdom @ Work*, Chip Conley shares the idea that companies will need wisdom coupled with fresh ideas. In 1987 at age 26, Conley founded a hotel and restaurant company and held the position of CEO for nearly 24 years. In 2010, after having created and managed 50 boutique hotels, he sold this business. In 2013, he was hired to consult with Airbnb, which had young founders and a fresh vibe. Conley loved the experience of working with the founders and their team. While he learned a lot, he was also able to share the experience and wisdom he had accumulated over decades in the accommodation industry that the younger founders simply didn't have. He was hired for his wisdom.

No matter how far artificial intelligence gets, it will never be able to replace empathy, real-life experience, or the creativity of the human mind. Conley has gone on to launch the Modern Elder Academy, the world's first midlife wisdom school, dedicated to navigating midlife transitions. The academy offers structured programming designed to help people think, feel, and explore their way through midlife.

The jobs that don't exist now are hard to define, but I think this leaves even more room for coming up with a job description that you like for yourself. There is plenty of room for creativity. As the economy changes, we'll likely be living a life of access instead of acquisition, meaning that we'll no longer feel the need to own things as much as we will need to have access to them. Cars are a prime example. With the growth of Lyft and Uber and the advent of driverless cars, people won't need to own their own vehicle, which means the expense of a car will disappear from their budgets. How will they want to spend that newfound discretionary income, and how can you be poised to meet that need?

Consider caretaking. We're all familiar with the idea of a caretaker who helps the disabled go to the bathroom or clean themselves, but what about simpler kinds of caretaking? Older generations might need online caretakers, people who help them manage their money online, pay bills, administer accounts—things they don't necessarily want to do or have the skill or patience for.

Jim Buckley ran a car dealership for the first half of his career, until he sold the business when he was 45 years old. Before doing so, he created an exit plan for himself. He was interested in the bail bonds business because it would allow him to stay engaged in work without the stressors of his previous job. So he started doing it on the weekends (which is prime time for a bail bondsman anyway). He experimented to see if he enjoyed the work before he committed to it. He went into his office for four or five hours a day, read his paper, and had the ultimate discretion over who he chose to work with—he felt good about taking on clients whom he felt would make good on the arrangement. At different points of his life, he did more work or less, depending on what suited him. Although he no longer does the work, it provided a bridge for him between his career and fully retired life.

A Silver Lining of COVID-19

The traditional full-time nine-to-five employee model was already starting to fade before the arrival of COVID, but the global lockdown really opened our eyes to what was possible in terms of work flexibility. Many companies are implementing hybrid models for their employees, giving them the option to work at the office or from home. According to Gallup's 2024 research, 53 percent of employees have some kind of hybrid work arrangement, and 27 percent are fully remote.[10] Additionally, many industries that primarily worked locally are now much more comfortable doing business virtually, with far fewer geographical constraints.

Take my financial services business for example. For the entirety of my career going back to 1998, I did face-to-face business with my clients. Fewer than 5 percent of them were not local, usually only because they were local to me at first and then moved away. Most people expected to have a relationship with a financial advisor they could meet in person. Since the lockdown forced us to work from home, I have received more referrals to clients who live in a different time zone than those who live close by. In fact, I recently received a referral to a physicians' practice in Hawaii. I was told that they had previously limited their options to someone on the island, but after a few less-than-ideal relationships—coupled with everyone doing business over Zoom—they were open to working with a firm farther away. Of course, despite meeting them under this premise, I assured them that if we start working together, I will be more than happy to travel to Hawaii once a year to meet with them in person. In 2023, I started offering to meet my clients in person again. Of all clients I conducted a review for in that year, only one asked to meet in the flesh.

Many companies will never go back to the traditional, in-person model. One of the main reasons for this is the massive savings from not having a hefty lease bill. One of the by-products of having more virtual employees is a company can hire the very best talent regardless of where they are located. This is great news if you are someone looking

If you are working in an industry you love, in a role you love, and with people you love, on your terms and timeline, why would you ever want to stop?

to work in a niche area, as you are no longer limited to the companies in your backyard. It is also great news if you have a business or will be starting one in the future. One of the primary reasons people do not like their job or industry—and why they would find a traditional retirement appealing—is they don't like the people they work with. Your pool of potential employees and clients will now cover the globe, which makes it far more likely that you will be able to attract and retain clients and employees whom you love to serve. If you are working in an industry you love, in a role you love, and with people you love, on your terms and timeline, why would you ever want to stop?

Start Now

If you currently have a job or own a business and are looking to transition to something else in the future, the best time to try out new skills and interests is while you have a reliable income stream. As Adam Grant shared in his book *Originals*, entrepreneurs have a reputation for being risk-takers, but in reality, many of the most successful entrepreneurs are very good risk-mitigators. Grant references a study involving over 5,000 Americans in their 20s, 30s, 40s, and 50s who became entrepreneurs. Some of these people maintained their existing job (and income) while others left it all behind to focus entirely on their new gig. Surprisingly, the study showed that entrepreneurs who kept their day jobs had 33 percent lower odds of failure than those who quit cold turkey.

Having some predictable income coming in the door affords you a lot of flexibility. If you are currently an employee who is interested in starting your own business (now or in the future) it may be harder than it needs to be if you have to rely on your new business to pay your bills. I believe the majority of problems in business, for both the client and the company providing the product or service, stem from the business owner or sales rep choosing to work with someone who is not a good fit for them.

This is one of the main reasons I decided to jettison most of my financial clients. No one likes saying no to a potential client, but there may be red flags if you look for them. Perhaps it's a potential customer who is asking for things that you currently do not provide, but they are willing to pay you a meaningful amount of money. Maybe you start working with someone and they become a PITA (Pain in the Ass), either by demanding more of your time, paying late, or something else. If this business is your only source of income, and you need the money to pay your mortgage, you will likely be making exceptions that, over time, will suck the joy out of you.

When you have some income coming in to cover your obligations, you won't have to compromise. You can set up your business to work with a specific type of person, who pays you to do specific things—and you can say no to anyone who isn't a great fit.

If you've made it this far, your wheels may be turning about what you could do in the next chapter of your life. Maybe you're even getting excited about the prospect of getting out of the job you're in now. That's great, and I hope you keep your excitement up. Consider ways to explore your career options, monetize the activities and hobbies you're most passionate about, and acquire new skills.

FINANCIAL PLANNING FOR NONTRADITIONAL RETIREES

{ 7 }

How to Set Up Your Financial Plan

I HOPE THAT by now, I've convinced you to rethink your plan and create a life so great you don't want to retire. In the second half of the book, I'll tell you how to construct a financial plan that works for you, and we'll dive deeper into each area of your plan. This section serves as a general overview. I don't go into every available financial instrument, nor do I explore everything in depth. I could write whole books on investment strategies, annuities, life insurance, estate planning, or tax-deferred savings. That's not the goal of this book; I want to give you high-level coverage of what I think you should consider when you build your financial plan. Specific advice tailored to your situation is far outside of the scope of this book, so make sure you seek advice from a qualified financial or legal expert before making any big decisions. I encourage you to find an advisor who will support this unconventional approach, but be aware that most of them are likely to be unfamiliar with it and might continue to provide traditional advice, even though it no longer applies to you.

In 25 years of advising clients, I've noticed that there are important pieces of a sound plan that many people consistently overlook. Regardless of how long you plan to work, I want to share with you a few things that will help ensure that your financial planning stays intact and will help minimize surprise expenses. I have tried to focus on traditional planning concepts that someone may want to reconsider once they acknowledge the likelihood of working beyond 65, as well as potentially significant strategies and conversations that are often overlooked. After you've gone through this material, consider having a conversation with a financial professional who can help you apply this guidance to your situation.

The next few chapters are going to be more technical than the rest of the book. They should be a great asset to you if you decide to opt out of the traditional approach to retirement. You may want to revisit them once you have had a chance to reconsider how your life (and planning) may change as a result of reading this book. Feel free to skip ahead to chapter 10 in the meantime. Having said that, I will be covering several concepts that will likely be new and beneficial to you, and they could make or save you a lot of money. If you do skip ahead, don't forget to return.

How to Think about Your Financial Plan: Focus on the Here and Now

When my clients and I go through their financial plan every year, I constantly preach noncommitment. Noncommitment to a certain number; noncommitment to one way of life. The goal is to show them where they're at just then, in that snapshot of time, in that year, so they have the information they need to make the best choices for themselves—whether they want to spend more, save more, or invest more. This approach forgoes a giant list of assumptions and asks them to focus on the here and now.

This approach offers the flexibility to adapt as life changes. This adaptability becomes especially important when we consider major life decisions, such as how we want our careers to adapt as we age. As soon as you go from asking yourself, "*When* do I want to retire?" to "*Do* I want to retire?" your financial plan, and life, changes radically. It should take into account where you are now, where you want to be in the future, and your desire to live a fulfilled and meaningful life.

In my opinion, a sound financial plan involves four key components:

1. Emergency savings
2. Mortgage and debt management
3. Insurance and investment plans
4. Estate planning

The overall thinking of the plan is laid out below.

1. Emergency Savings

First, start with building up six months' worth of expenses in an account that is easily reachable, and not subject to volatility. You should likely do this before you fund investment plans—with the exception of 401(k) contributions that are matched by your employer. The reason for an emergency savings account is to prevent you from having to pull money from your investment accounts if the timing is not ideal. If you're putting money exclusively into investments that have the potential for volatility and your car breaks down or one of your parents has a health issue during a dip in the market, you will be in a less-than-ideal situation. And if the only money you have to your name is in a retirement plan, and you need to withdraw from it, you'll potentially incur a 10 percent penalty, as well as income taxes. A sound financial plan includes minimizing the effect of any life events that might introduce short-term volatility and risk. As long as you never have to sell investments when the market is down, any market contractions or volatility are only losses on paper. You don't want to be in a position to have to sell for cash when the market is down, which is why you need an emergency savings account.

Now, the amount you set aside isn't set in stone. For some people, six months' worth of expenses is just right. Others won't be comfortable unless they have a year's worth saved up. If you have a low cost of living or have other pools of non-restricted money you can pull from, you might need less. Think through your potential short-term cash needs and set aside an amount that won't severely restrict your spending or draw from accounts that penalize you for doing so. Is your car brand new, or did it just hit the 100,000-mile mark? Are you renting, or did you buy an older home that may need its roof replaced soon? These are some examples to consider.

You should also consider the "sleep at night" factor. What amount of emergency savings will help you sleep better knowing that you have it tucked away? Better yet, what amount will no longer cause the worry tab in your brain to constantly run in the background? Work toward building that emergency stash up before you move on to the next step.

2. Mortgage and Debt Management

It's advice you hear from everyone, and most financial plans are built on the assumption that you'll follow it: pay down your debts and your mortgage so you no longer have to deal with the payments when you retire. Just like the general notion of saving for traditional retirement, people follow this advice blindly without thinking too deeply about it.

Debt has become a negative word. The financial industry focuses on paying down debt at all costs. But there is good debt and there is bad debt, and it's important to incorporate your debt into your overall financial plan in a way that takes advantage of your opportunities and minimizes your losses.

This is my overall thesis on handling debt: To decide whether to keep a debt, consider the opportunity cost—what else you could do with the money, and what is the potential return on those alternatives? Ask yourself if it makes sense to continue to take your time paying it off, or would it be better if you aggressively paid it down? If you can get a higher rate of return by taking your money and putting it somewhere else, then you should do so. If you can't get a return that will match or come close to the interest rate, then you should aggressively pay down that debt.

Think about the interest rate on your debt as a guaranteed rate of return. For example, if you pay off a loan or a portion of a loan that has a 7 percent interest rate, it's effectively the same as earning a 7 percent return on an investment. By paying down the loan, you're avoiding the cost of future interest payments, which is comparable to earning an equivalent return on an investment. Getting a guaranteed rate of 7 percent annually (by paying off debt with a 7 percent interest rate) is a return that is hard to beat. However, if the interest rate is significantly lower than that, it might not make sense to be in a hurry to pay down debt if you can likely earn a better rate of return elsewhere.

There are some clear examples of debt you might want to pay off as soon as possible. Obviously, credit card debt—particularly when you're paying 15 to 30 percent on consumer items—is bad debt. The math doesn't work out; you're paying opportunity costs for what you could be earning on that money if you were to invest it instead of paying down the debt.

Should I Pay Down My Mortgage? Not Necessarily

Advisors, banks, and mortgage specialists have preached for years to pay down your mortgage because they suggest this is the safe, conservative, and responsible thing to do. When you pay off your mortgage, you fulfill the American dream. There is also some peace of mind that comes from owning a house mortgage-free because it gives you the feeling that no one can take it away from you. This craving for peace of mind stems from the Depression era. At the time, most mortgages were callable loans, meaning that banks could go to a homeowner and, out of nowhere, say, "You owe us X amount of money on this house, and we want you to pay the entire balance right now." Nonpayment meant losing the house, but few people had thousands of dollars to pay off the bank on a moment's notice. That's the reason a lot of people lost their homes, which created a lot of generational trauma. The laws have changed, and banks can't do that anymore, but we still have this primal fear of being kicked off our land, so we strive to pay the house off—even if it's not in our best interest financially.

One point I want to clarify is that a homeowner will fully participate in the appreciation of their home, regardless of how much principal they have paid. Let's say someone buys a $1 million home and puts down 20 percent while another person buys another $1 million home and puts down 40 percent. One year from now the homes are appraised at $1.1 million. Each person has increased their net worth by $100,000. In fact, the person who put down less got a higher rate of return. They also had more money to invest elsewhere if they chose. I wanted to make this point because of the misconception

Choosing *not* to aggressively pay down your mortgage could give you much more flexibility to access your money.

that when you pay down the principal on your home loan, it equates to investing in your home. In reality, any money you pay to reduce the principal, above and beyond your monthly mortgage payment, is the equivalent to putting it under your mattress. The only effect is that you shorten the time you will have to make payments.

Given what I just shared about debt, instead of aggressively paying down your mortgage, consider whether there are other investment vehicles available that would pay you more than the interest of the mortgage. If you can invest that money where it will likely earn more, you shouldn't be in a big hurry to pay off your mortgage. As of this writing, I have a 3 percent fixed mortgage, and I am earning 5 percent in a money market account. Paying anything above the minimum on my mortgage payment out of this money market account will cost me money.

Now, there are some important reasons to consider continuing to carry a mortgage, even if you think you can afford to pay it off, especially for those who will continue to work into their later years. One of the many reasons home ownership has grown in popularity in the US over the past 50 years is because of the tax deduction that comes along with it. If your mortgage rate is 5 percent and you're in a 40 percent tax bracket, your net rate could be 3 percent in the early years, because you're able to write off the interest you are paying.

For most people, the mortgage deduction is the best tax break they have access to. If you've aggressively paid off your mortgage and find yourself in your 70s, still earning an income, you no longer get that tax deduction. You will not only pay more in taxes, but you will also increase the likelihood that you're going to be in a higher marginal tax rate, because you can no longer leverage the best tax deduction available to you.

Choosing *not* to aggressively pay down your mortgage could give you much more flexibility to access your money.

3. Insurance and Investment Plans

We'll talk more about these two options in later chapters, but in terms of your overall financial plan, know that you'll need to protect yourself and your family against unforeseen events that could wreak havoc on your lives. Having good insurance coverage in place is an important part of minimizing risk and volatility. You'll want a good strategy for your investments. I'll help you think about how you've diversified your investments not only across asset classes but across tax buckets.

Taking advantage of your employer-sponsored 401(k), especially if there are matching funds, is the first low-hanging fruit to address. You should also think about the money you might need in two to five years. Things that fall into that category include planning for a job transition and the need to take time off, buying a second home, or taking an extended trip somewhere. If you know you have a big event on the horizon, you don't want that money subjected to the ups and downs of the market, and you also don't want it locked into a retirement plan with penalties for withdrawing. Consider setting that money aside and investing very conservatively, so that it still earns a return in the interim. You want to be flexible with that money, and you want it to earn some interest.

After you create your emergency savings, choose how you will handle debt, get the insurance plans you need, and allocate your investments across tax buckets, your plan can go in a lot of different directions depending on your needs. If you have kids, the next batch of money might be put toward saving for their college education. If you know you'll want to make a career transition or invest in a business, you'll want to set money aside for those endeavors.

Have the Important Conversations

One of the most important things I do is encourage my clients to have a conversation with their parents to discuss how they will be cared for as they age. Most people have no clue about the state of their parents' finances. That's a major problem if you know that you'll be the one to step in and help them out if they face some kind of challenge later in life.

For example, if one of your parents needs intensive daily medical care, or requires a long-term nursing facility, and they don't have long-term care insurance, who will foot the bill? If you will be the one, you will want to know that well in advance so you can factor it into your plan.

Fortunately, I did this with my parents. I recognized that some of the financial burden of my parents' care—should they need it—would fall on me, and I sat them down around the dining room table to talk about their money. Afterward, I helped them get a long-term care insurance plan in place that ultimately saved them millions of dollars over the nine-year period when my father had dementia. If we hadn't done that in advance, my mother would be broke right now. Having that plan allowed her to retain the hard-earned money they had invested over the years. It also prevented any negative consequences to my own financial plan.

If you haven't done this yet, it's time to have a conversation with your parents about their savings, their insurance plans, and the way they view their future. You may hesitate about broaching this topic because it doesn't seem like your business, but at the end of the day, if you are going to be using your money to help them in a health or financial crunch, it *is* your business, and you want to know that information as soon as possible.

It might not be easy to bring up the topic of money with your parents. Given that I was their financial advisor and already managed their money, it was relatively easy for me to broach the topic, but I recognize this is probably not the case for everybody. Here are some talking points to get you started.

Start discussions early. Don't wait until they're in financial trouble to have a conversation. Having a conversation after a major diagnosis or emergency might make it harder for everyone to remain calm.

Choose your wording. Parents might find it hard to have a conversation with adult children about finances, particularly if they're embarrassed by the topic. Reinforce the idea that you're trying to help them and share with them any plans you've made around your own financial future, especially where it concerns them. For example, if you're setting aside money for them, sharing that news might open the door for them to share.

Ask them about their wishes for their retirement years and their end-of-life plans. They probably have ideas and preferences about how the end of their lives will go, and if you start the conversation by letting them talk openly, they'll be more likely to feel as though you've understood. Also ask them about how they prefer to spend the last few years of their lives. Will they want to live with you or another family member? Do they have long-term care or a preference about the kind of home they may go to?

Try to get the full financial picture. Can they afford retirement? Do they currently have any debt? Will they need financial help? What insurance policies are in place? Is there a will and estate plan in place? Who is the designated power of attorney, and the executor for the will? If they don't know or seem unsure, or if there are important pieces of their plan that haven't been addressed, assure them that's okay and you will help them figure it out.

Get clear on documentation. Is there a place where all passwords are located should something happen to them? Where can you find information on their financial accounts?

Ask if there's anything in the will that might cause friction between siblings or family members.

Finally, plan for future conversations. Even if the conversation didn't go quite as well as you hoped, thank them for sitting down to talk to you about their finances, tell them what you plan to do to follow up (if necessary), and suggest that you have another check-in conversation within a short period of time. If they were less than forthcoming, your calm response will reassure them that you're there to help them and might encourage them to open up more next time you broach this topic.

Talking Money with Your Spouse or Life Partner

As important as it is to talk about finances with your parents, it's even more important to be on the same page with your spouse or life partner. You would be surprised how often couples lack alignment in their finances—I notice that many of them talk about their plan really only once a year, when they sit down to talk to their financial advisor.

When I say alignment, I don't mean that they agree on everything about money. In my opinion, the best relationships are those where one person is a spender, and one person is a saver. If they were both spenders, they would go broke; if they were both savers, they would have a boring relationship. There's always going to be some give-and-take in the way couples invest and spend. As long as they both trust me to give the right advice, their differences in spending or saving don't have to be a roadblock. However, when a couple is not in alignment about an overall plan or about trusting me (or their financial advisor) to administer the plan, I see this as a red flag.

If you haven't talked finances with your spouse recently, or sense you aren't aligned on your financial plan, starting that conversation is one of the most important steps you can take. If you find it hard to talk to your spouse about money, this is not unusual; it is one of the main reasons people go to couples' therapy. You're not alone. The hardships of financial conversations between spouses could fill a book, which is one of the reasons I'm not concerned about AI taking over for financial advisors. Guiding couples on complex financial decisions is a core value that good advisors provide—and a machine will (likely) never replace. If you and your partner strongly disagree, I might suggest first finding a couples' counselor to work with before doing any heavy lifting on your financial plan. Then look for a financial advisor that you both can agree to trust.

I spend a lot of time vetting the people I'm going to hire or who will give me professional advice. I want to know who they are, how they think, and their track record of success. Once I feel good about whom I'm working with, I let go and trust them and their recommendations because I feel confident in the work I did up front to make sure I hired someone who will help me support my goals.

My hope is that you and your partner can agree on what it is you're looking for in an advisor, feel confident about vetting them, and then agree to trust their advice. A good advisor will take both of your needs, worries, and goals into consideration when making suggestions. I've had to navigate a few difficult client relationships, but for the most part, couples take my advice because they trust me. It's less about how to work with your significant other in that case, and more about finding the right person to work with and guide you both through your financial plan.

Remember, at the end of the day, this isn't about following my advice to a T. I want you to focus on flexibility and

Way too many people don't have a will or an estate plan in place because they get overwhelmed by the decisions they have to make.

diversity of your assets to serve what you want in life, rather than finding the "right" way to do it.

4. Estate Planning

Right up there with emergency savings is the need to put a will, and potentially trusts, in place to ensure the assets you've worked hard to accumulate are distributed the way you want when you die, or when both you and your spouse pass away. I will say up front, however, that if you're single or married without any children, I don't think you need to spend a lot of time carving out your estate plan. However, you could consider nieces and nephews or other family members to whom you might want to leave money or assets.

The larger your estate, the more planning you will need to consider. If you have children, there are two essential items to address sooner rather than later: who will be the guardians of your kids if something happens to you and their other parent, and who is going to oversee the assets to make sure they are used in a responsible way for the benefit of your children.

In my experience, way too many people don't have a will or an estate plan in place because they get overwhelmed by the decisions they have to make. Deciding who will raise their kids in the event they die is not a light topic by any stretch of the imagination, so many parents put off doing it entirely because they can't decide, or because the conversation causes a lot of friction in their relationship. As uncomfortable as it may be to have these discussions and make these decisions, avoiding them can create significantly negative consequences for your children and estate. Without planning in advance, the estate will likely enter probate, potentially leaving it in limbo for months or even years and eroding its value by upwards of approximately 30 percent due to legal and court fees.

If you don't decide who will be the guardians of your children before your untimely death, the court will decide for you after your passing. They will essentially ask for volunteers to take over for you in the child-rearing department. Hopefully your sister and your co-parent's brother get along great and both agree that one would be better in this role than the other, and of course, all of the other siblings, grandparents, and so on agree with this choice as well. However, this isn't usually how it goes down. Oftentimes, multiple people think they would be ideal for the role and there is a fight in court to see who wins. This never ends well, especially not for your kids. You need to deal with the uncomfortableness of the conversation now to make sure your kids end up with the best guardians for *them*.

Melanie and I have gone back and forth over our kids' guardians many times, and for us it's a conversation that's never over. People change over the years—as our boys grow and we realize who they are becoming, we have to reevaluate who would be the best guardian for them. I don't want to overcomplicate your decision with too many considerations, but my wife and I believe the primary consideration should not solely be who loves them most, but also who can provide a life that most closely matches what they would have experienced with us. This perspective shifts the focus from familial ties alone to a more comprehensive view of your child's overall well-being and continuity of life experience.

Consider broadening your scope when you consider guardians. Your relatives may be very loving, warm people, but their values and the way they go about living their lives might be very different from yours. Some people in your life might not seem like obvious choices. Don't limit yourself to family members but look for those in your close inner circle whom you would trust to raise your child the way you would: with love and similar values. The aim is to ensure that your children continue to live in an environment that reflects the principles, beliefs, and quality of life you prioritize. Initiating conversations, exploring their openness to the role, and discussing your expectations can reveal potential guardians who are capable and willing to provide for your child in ways that align closely with your own parenting approach.

Finding the Right Person to Look After Your Money
The second item you'll want to address now involves the money and assets you will leave behind. The primary reason to address this right now is to avoid a scenario where your children will receive large sums of money on their 18th birthday, which is an age that is not typically correlated with making good financial decisions.

Whomever you choose as the custodian of your money may be different from the person you choose as the guardian of your children. However you divide responsibility, you want a plan that minimizes expenses and maximizes the effectiveness of the ways your kids can use the money in a manner that won't ruin their lives.

We established specific milestones and ages for when our children can access funds for particular reasons; they receive a certain amount at 18 and can access funds to buy a home at 25. They will also have access to funds for their education, as well as the opportunity to pitch their business ideas to a "financial board" composed of my business partner, my brother, and a close family friend. If at least two board members approve, the funds can be allocated for their proposed venture instead of education.

This approach is not typical, but it underscores the importance of planning how and when your children will access their inheritance to prevent potential mismanagement. Children don't typically handle exorbitant amounts of money well. This is why it's important to consult with an estate planning attorney to create a comprehensive plan. This ensures your children's inheritance is distributed in a manner that supports their well-being and financial stability and aligns with their life events, age milestones, or achievements. This will mitigate the risk of them potentially misusing a large sum at a young age.

Estate planning also gives you the opportunity to make important decisions about your care preferences should you become unable to make them yourself. This provided incredible comfort for us when my father's health declined. When he reached the point where he could no longer eat and needed a feeding tube installed, we consulted his medical directive, which clearly stated his wish to avoid any measures aimed at solely prolonging his life under those circumstances. This helped us align our decisions with his desires at a time when he couldn't communicate them. This aspect of estate planning underscores the importance of documenting your care preferences to ensure they are honored, offering peace of mind to both you and your family.

AS YOU'VE SEEN, planning for a fulfilling and financially sustainable life involves challenging conventional ideas about retirement. The traditional path may not fit everyone, and crafting a unique approach that blends financial security with a meaningful life can lead to greater satisfaction now and later. In the next section, we'll dive deeper into the practicalities of building a financial plan that aligns with your vision. Remember, this journey is about designing a life so fulfilling that retirement becomes less of a finish line and more of a natural evolution. Seek guidance wisely and embrace the opportunity to forge your own path.

{ 8 }

Insurance: Protection for the Future

IF YOU PLAN to work into your 70s and beyond, you will need to take a different approach to your insurance needs than someone planning for a traditional retirement. I want to make sure that you have appropriate levels of protection in place, in case the unexpected happens. Considering your unique situation and goals, assessing your insurance options, and customizing a plan is an important part of having a strong financial foundation.

Insurance helps mitigate the financial risks we all face in life—whether it's the risk of outliving savings, getting injured or too sick to work, or needing long-term care. By paying relatively small, predictable premiums, insurance protects you from large, unpredictable losses should life throw a curveball your way. The right insurance coverage gives you peace of mind, allowing you to focus on work and other priorities knowing you and your family have a safety net in place.

Life Insurance

The primary reason most people need life insurance is to replace their income in the event they die prematurely. If you're married and have children, and you're the only one earning an income, your spouse would be at an obvious disadvantage if you died and were no longer earning money. Even if you both work, you likely depend on both incomes. Life insurance helps to ensure that your spouse, family, and dependents will not have to suffer or change the plans in place should you pass away unexpectedly.

In this section, I'll show you how to determine how much life insurance you may need and the differences between term and whole life insurance.

Considering What You Need

You can sit down with your financial advisor or an insurance agent and get as detailed as you want, but a good rule of thumb—no matter what kind of life insurance you choose—is to leave an amount of money that is able to grow *and* provide income for your family when it's invested in a responsible way. The equation for how much insurance you need is very similar to the equation used to determine how much money you need to retire (using the traditional model).

Assuming the lump sum payout will grow annually at a rate of 6 to 7 percent, your family should be able to safely withdraw 4 to 5 percent without the risk of eroding the principal. Essentially, for every $50,000 of annual income you want to replace in the event you die prematurely, you will need to leave behind approximately $1 million in assets or insurance proceeds. (It is also likely you will need to account for lump sum amounts that will need to be available right away, to fund college education for your children or pay off debt.)

For example, if you want to make sure your family will have $250,000 a year to live on should you pass away, then you want the total of your assets plus life insurance to equal roughly $5 million. With that amount, your family should be able to take $250,000 out each year without eroding the principal.

As for types of insurance, the difference between term and whole life is often described as *renting* insurance versus *owning* insurance, respectively. So which is best for you? There is no straightforward answer. It depends on your goals and needs, your ability to commit to whole life insurance (more on that in a moment), and where you might invest the difference. What works for one person won't work for another, so it's important to weigh the benefits of each.

Term Life Insurance

Term insurance is an inexpensive way to ensure that your family will be provided for in the unlikely event you pass away prematurely. When considering term insurance, you'll need to decide how long the coverage should last. Term life policies are most commonly sold in lengths of 5, 10, 15, 20, or 30 years. The longer the policy, the higher your monthly premiums. That's because you're locking in your rate for a longer term, and as you age, health problems tend to crop up and your likelihood of dying increases.

Twenty-year term life insurance is the most popular term length and can help cover the income of new parents or newlyweds as their family grows. A 5- or 10-year term life insurance policy may benefit parents who are late to planning for this need, those with older children who still rely on their income, or someone with obligations that lasted longer than originally expected. A 30-year policy should be strongly considered to cover any obligations that could last that long.

Term insurance policies are unilateral contracts, meaning the insurance company will guarantee the coverage at the offered rate for the length of the term as long as you continue to pay, but you can stop paying without ramifications (aside from losing the insurance).

In the traditional financial planning model, most people elect to start out with a 20-year term policy. If you are 40 years old with two small children, you will likely need insurance to get you through the next 20 years. When you are 60, your children (now adults) should no longer be dependent on you or in need of your income in the event you pass away. When your children are toddlers, it is unlikely that you have set much aside to fund their college education. You will need to make sure you have enough life insurance to fund this expense if you die while they are young. When they are 16 to 20 years old, you will hopefully have saved enough to cover the cost of their education and will no longer need to rely on life insurance to cover this expense.

The same logic (and math) applies for funding a traditional retirement. If you were planning to retire at 65 before reading this book, you should be saving an amount each year to arrive at a lump sum amount that will provide you and your spouse with what you need to live on in retirement. If you die prematurely, you will want to make sure you have enough life insurance to cover the gap that would have been filled by your savings. If you live a full life, or at least get to age 65, you will hopefully have saved enough so that you will no longer need life insurance to supplement your savings.

If you plan to work into your 70s and opt for term life insurance, you may need to extend your coverage longer to financially protect your family should something unexpectedly happen to you. Since you'll still be relying on earned income to cover some of your needs, your spouse may need life insurance to replace the loss of your income should you pass away unexpectedly.

The primary advantage of term insurance is its affordability—if you're healthy. When you apply for life insurance, you will be subject to a medical exam and a review of your health history. If you are 30 or 40, it is likely you're in good shape and will be given a rate based on your current health. However, the reason it's so cheap when compared to other types of policies is because you are likely (and hopefully) throwing this money away. The insurance companies (who understand death better than anyone) charge an affordable rate that's easy to pay because they know it's extremely unlikely that they will ever have to pay you.

A major disadvantage of term insurance is that if you want to extend your coverage beyond your term length, you will need to reapply. If you set up a 20-year policy at 35 and are now 55 and feel as though you still need insurance, you will now have to pay a 55-year-old's rate, which is a lot higher than the 35-year-old's rate. This of course assumes you qualify after going through another compulsory medical exam.

Whole Life Insurance

While there are other types of life insurance, the only other one I will discuss in this book is whole life insurance. The primary differences between term and whole life insurance are cost and length. Term life insurance is cheaper and covers you for a set period of time. Whole life insurance typically lasts your entire life and can build cash value, which makes it a more complex and expensive product. Whole life insurance is a viable option, but whether it's a good choice depends heavily on your situation. Although it's more complicated than term life insurance, whole life insurance is more straightforward than other types of permanent life insurance.

Some of the pros include premiums that remain level, a cash value that grows at a guaranteed fixed rate, and a death benefit that is guaranteed to be paid when you die (whenever that may be).

Many whole life insurance policies are set up with mutual companies (not stock companies), which means you may earn dividends based on the company's financial performance. You can use your dividends in a few different ways, including boosting your policy's cash value. The money inside the cash value of these policies can grow tax-free and in a way that doesn't correlate with the stock market. You can also borrow from these policies and use that money however you please, so they can be set up to be an alternative to some of the funds you would keep in a bank or bonds.

Now for the cons: Whole life insurance can be risky because of the required commitment to a specific payment over an extended period of time. This is not like your 401(k) plan, where you can turn off contributions whenever you want. When you buy whole life insurance, you commit to making the same payment on a monthly or annual basis for a minimum of 10 years, but ideally 20 years or longer. If for any reason you can no longer make those payments in the early years, any money you've put into the policy is essentially a donation to the life insurance company—you'll lose the policy, the money can't be recouped, and you won't be able to get the benefits. Anyone who buys this kind of insurance policy must feel extremely confident they'll be able to continue contributing the same amount for an extended period of time. As an advisor, I would want to know quite a lot about your situation before I suggest you buy a whole life insurance policy, because I wouldn't want you to make a horrible financial mistake for lack of understanding the commitment and your ability (or lack thereof) to follow through.

Planning to work into your 70s and beyond? You will need to take a different approach to your insurance needs than someone planning for a traditional retirement.

Like everything else in this book, this may not apply to everyone, so be sure you talk to your financial advisor or a qualified life insurance agent.

Disability Insurance

Though you probably don't expect to die anytime soon, there is a much greater (but still small) chance that you are going to experience some type of disability at some point while you're working. The primary purpose of disability insurance is to insure your income should such an unfortunate event occur.

Most of us probably think, *This will never happen to me.* But studies show that over 36 million Americans, roughly 12 percent or one in eight people, classify as disabled.[1] Of those, half are between the ages of 18 and 64. While people believe that their chance of long-term disability during their working years is 1 to 2 percent, this is far from the case: about one in four of today's 20-somethings will become disabled before they retire.[2] And the average disability lasts for two-and-a-half years.[3] If you suffer from some type of a disability that requires doctor visits, hospital stays, physical or occupational therapy, or medication, your health insurance is going to cover many of those expenses, but it will not pay your mortgage, your child's private school education, or your electric bills. That's where a disability insurance policy comes in. It ensures your paycheck so that if you can't work, you'll still be able to have an income until you're able to return to work.

Disability insurance is even more important for somebody who is planning to work beyond the traditional retirement age. As we've discussed, if someone is going the traditional route, they'll likely have more money saved up by the age of 60 than someone who has chosen to continue to work. If you're in the latter camp, your ability to continue to earn an income is a bigger factor for you than it is for them.

There are generally two options for disability insurance: short term and long term. Short-term disability typically covers a period of disability lasting up to six months and pays a portion of your income while you recover. This is the kind of coverage you'll find offered by most employers. With long-term disability, the coverage period usually kicks in at six months. Some of the more generous policies will pay benefits until retirement age. This insurance can protect your income for the long haul.

There are a couple of factors to consider. First, you'll want to think about the portion of income you want to replace. Policies pay a percentage of your gross income, often around 60 percent, which means you'll need to choose coverage that helps you maintain your lifestyle and have enough set aside to cover the gap. The benefit payment duration will impact the cost of the plan. Shorter benefit periods cost less; longer benefits periods cost more.

Second, make sure you understand how the policy defines "disability." Each policy might define a qualifying disability differently, and you don't want to be left with a restrictive policy and no income. You may want a more liberal policy that offers more coverage and a wider definition of a qualifying disability. Related to this, consider buying a policy that covers disabilities stemming from mental illness, which is far more common than you might think. Many policies also offer the option to add a rider to protect your benefit from inflation. Finally, one of the upsides to getting disability insurance is that benefits are generally tax-free if you paid the premiums yourself on an after-tax basis (which is what I always recommend).

Long-Term Care Insurance

Long-term care insurance provides care for you should you have some kind of health condition that requires you to be in a nursing home or have a professional caretaker. Eligibility requirements can vary between companies and plans. Some of the factors they consider include the following.

- Age: Most plans have age limits for enrollment, with the upper limit often being 75 years of age.

- Health status: Most plans will take into consideration pre-existing health conditions that may impact your premium costs. At the time that you apply, there may be questions about your ability to perform daily living tasks.

- Personal or family medical history: Companies will ask about your family's history of medical conditions such as Alzheimer's disease.

There are no standard set criteria that will definitively determine your eligibility, and the criteria can vary between insurance companies. An expert insurance agent can help navigate what requirements different carriers may have.

If you have the forethought to put this in place, it can be a huge boon to your savings. The statistics are staggering. According to a 2022 US Department of Health and Human Services study, about 64 percent of women and 49 percent of men who reach the age of 65 will require long-term care at some point during their later years.[4] The typical need for long-term care insurance is about three years. Why three years? Because many people who use long-term care insurance do so because they have a health condition that will eventually kill them, such as cancer or heart disease.

Again, your health insurance is going to pay your primary medical bills, and your disability insurance is going to replace your income. But long-term care insurance would pay for a nurse to come to your home a couple of times a week, or it would help offset the cost of going into a nursing home, which can start at $4,000 and go beyond $10,000 per month, depending on the needs and the facility—and it's far more expensive if you need memory care.

Like disability insurance, long-term care insurance has waiting periods and limitations on how long the benefit lasts. For example, the standard disability insurance or long-term care insurance has a 90-day wait, which is like the equivalent of a deductible with your auto insurance. In other words, they expect that if you can't work for 90 days, you've got enough saved up in the bank to cover your expenses for three months. If you're still disabled beyond 90 days, that's when your insurance will kick in. You can certainly get insurance that will kick in after 30 days, but the extra cost is typically not money well spent in my opinion.

Anyone can apply for long-term care insurance, but there are a few things you need to keep in mind. First, you likely don't need to think about buying this kind of policy until you're between 50 and 55 years old. The odds are very good that you'll pay for time that is, in a way, unnecessary (and for single folks without families, I personally wouldn't even bother with it). Second, no matter where you buy the policy, you are unlikely to get a guaranteed premium. You'll pay a certain amount of money for your long-term care insurance, and the amount you have to pay will likely go up eventually. Typically, insurance companies can't arbitrarily raise rates. If you've bought one version of an insurance package, you're set with that benefit, unless the amount of the benefit they're paying out to insured people of that specific version becomes high enough relative to the premiums they collect. When that happens, the insurance company will go to the state commissioners and ask to raise the rates. Only if the company

I consider dementia and Alzheimer's to be the greatest threat to your financial plan.

can demonstrate the need will they then be allowed to raise rates. With most of these policies, you'll still get some benefit on a prorated basis relative to the amount you contributed, but it likely won't be what you signed up to receive if you stop making payments at some point.

The kind of long-term care policy I bought for myself and recommend for the majority of my clients allows me to prepay or guarantee payments for a period of time that will not be subject to future rate increases. It is guaranteed because it is a hybrid long-term care and life insurance policy. With some hybrid policies, you can pay a one-time premium that's fully guaranteed, although they come at a steep cost. You can also opt for payments over various lengths of time and cost depending on your needs.

This won't be applicable to everyone, but I mention it to every one of my clients, even those who are in very good shape: I consider dementia and Alzheimer's to be the greatest threat to your financial plan. Again, because you can live with them for a long time. You can have everything clicking with your financial plan, and if you get diagnosed with some form of dementia and don't have long-term care insurance, or your spouse gets it, you're going to use a lot of your assets to pay for care. Unless you've been through it yourself, or have watched a family member or close friend go through it, it's hard to appreciate how much this can deplete your assets.

If you don't think you need long-term care insurance for yourself just yet, you may want to consider whether your parents will need it. As we discussed in chapter 7, if your mother or father were to develop a debilitating disease, how likely is that you would step in to take care of them? If you feel like that burden would fall on you, it will probably make sense to get long-term care insurance for your parents.

I thank God I had this conversation with my parents early on and got a very good long-term care policy in place before my father got dementia. If I hadn't done that, one of two things would have happened: My mother would have had to care for my dad by herself; she might have gone mad with the weight of responsibility and my father wouldn't have gotten the level of care he needed. Or, she would have aggressively spent down everything they had saved over the years. Instead, my mom received $300 per day in the form of a daily benefit, which meant she had more than enough funds to pay for high-quality care for my dad. Someone came to the house six days a week for a few hours a day early on to look after him; eventually, a nurse was there 24-7. This arrangement provided a better quality of life for both of them. The burden of being the sole caretaker is exponential. The mental and emotional burdens take their toll, and often caretakers don't get the time and space they need to take care of themselves.

Health Insurance

Health insurance is difficult to talk about in this book, given that there are so many options based on where you live and whether or not you are traditionally employed or own your own business. However, I will say that one of the advantages of working beyond the traditional retirement age is that you are typically going to have access to much better health insurance—or at least much better rates for health insurance—than you would if you were on your own and responsible for getting a personal policy.

If you run a company and you have group health insurance that you provide for your employees, you can continue to participate in that program. If you're an employee of another company that provides great benefits, you get to maintain that coverage while you're working there. As of this writing, the individual private market is much more expensive, and it's much harder for people to get coverage that way.

Liability Insurance

You probably don't need me to tell you that regardless of your plans for retirement, you want to have adequate insurance in place when it comes to your home and your car. But there are a couple of things that a lot of people fail to plan for, and I'm going to share them here.

The underlying theme of insurance is protection against a big catastrophic event and a guarantee that you don't lose all your money when it could have been prevented. Having said that, most people shop for car insurance by being price sensitive and paying the minimum that's required for coverage. In a lot of cases that's perfectly fine, and you can make plenty of arguments over what your deductible should or shouldn't be. One thing I want to highlight is a line item within your auto insurance called "uninsured/under-insured" coverage.

One out of eight, or 12 percent, of drivers in the United States don't have auto insurance.[5] If you're in a car accident with somebody who does not have insurance, and the accident is their fault and you end up badly injured and/or your car gets wrecked, you will not get any money from them. Even if they have coverage that gives a very low payout, you won't get enough to cover all the repairs and damage you suffered as a result of the accident. When you have uninsured/under-insured coverage, your policy will kick in and pay you the money in the event the other driver doesn't have coverage or doesn't have adequate coverage. Most people don't have that kind of insurance, and they don't know it's a major factor in auto accidents.

For example, the minimum insurance coverage required in most US states is $25,000 bodily injury liability per person; $50,000 bodily injury liability per accident; and $25,000 property damage liability per accident.[6] However, you can and likely should bump these numbers up to $100,000 for injury to one person in an accident and $300,000 per accident. The difference in cost will be nominal for most people and yet it makes a very big difference in the financial outcome of a car accident.

Additionally, you need to consider having general liability insurance, which can be combined with your homeowner's insurance. Otherwise known as an umbrella policy, liability insurance is good to have in the event you are sued for an accident on your property. Incidents covered could include something as straightforward as somebody slipping in your driveway and breaking their neck. They might be left with high medical bills for the next 20 years and they could technically sue you for that, and you could lose all the money you've worked so hard to save to pay their medical bills. This scenario doesn't apply to everyone, but if you own a home, it makes sense to have liability coverage.

Do you ever text while you're driving? An unfortunately realistic scenario is one where you hit someone while you're texting and driving. If you don't have liability insurance and the person you hit suffers a lot of health problems because of the accident, you could find yourself filing for bankruptcy and losing everything you've saved up to that point, plus a good bit of your future earnings. You can get good liability coverage, which might cover up to $5 million in damages, for as little as $500 a year. It's not very expensive, and it'll make sure that you get to retain your assets in the event of a worst-case scenario.

Having the right insurance coverage, customized to your situation, provides important financial protection when the unexpected happens. When you take the time up front to assess risks and align the right policies with your goals and needs, you can have peace of mind that you and your loved ones are safe from unnecessary financial strain. This shores up your underlying financial foundation and allows you to focus energy on finding and creating a life that fulfills and satisfies you well into your later years.

{ 9 }

Investment Strategies

WHEN IT comes to investing and saving for retirement, most people primarily focus on how much they should invest and what their rate of return will be. While these are certainly important, there are a few other important considerations that will greatly impact your plan. In this chapter, I will discuss the best allocation of your savings across different account types to minimize taxes, the appropriate balance of risk in your investments as you age, strategies to optimize required minimum distributions, and the power of working just a few years longer.

The following strategies will provide flexibility to adjust your financial plan as you see fit, ensuring your goals align with the way you want to spend your time. I don't want you to feel the need to adhere to a strict plan, but I do want you to have a good idea of how short-term choices will impact you later in life. Remember, the goal isn't a rigid, long-term financial commitment that you must adhere to no matter what—the goal is also to live fully in the here and now. By embracing a dynamic approach, you can better navigate the uncertainties of life and find greater peace and fulfillment now and later.

Many people do not properly account for all of these elements, but they can have an incredible impact on the end result of your plan. Failing to diversify your tax exposure, manage risk, coordinate distributions, and leverage the ability to work longer can have you running out of money. By better understanding these key pillars and taking a more comprehensive approach, you will be setting yourself up for a more secure and sustainable future.

Your Investment Plan Options

A well-planned strategy requires that you understand the different kinds of savings vehicles available and diversify across these options in a way that supports you as much as possible. I am going to provide you with an overview of some of these vehicles, and then we'll dig into the best ways to use each of them.

If you have spent any time working in the US, then it is very likely you have contributed money to a 401(k) plan. To refresh what we covered earlier, this kind of retirement savings plan offered by many American employers has some advantages for the saver. The employee with a traditional 401(k) agrees to have a percentage of pre-tax wages withdrawn from their paycheck and paid directly into an investment account. The employer may match part or all of that contribution. The employee gets to choose among a number of investment options within that 401(k) plan, usually mutual funds. Any money invested in a 401(k) plan should be viewed as money you will not need to use for a long time. If you want to withdraw funds from your 401(k) plan prior to age 59½, that money will be subject to tax, and you will be hit with a 10 percent early distribution penalty.

Another traditional retirement vehicle used by many Americans is an individual retirement account (IRA). The main difference between 401(k)s and IRAs is that 401(k)s are offered through employers whereas IRAs are opened by individuals through an advisor or a bank. IRAs are also the place where someone can move their 401(k) after they leave their employer. With both traditional 401(k) plans and traditional IRAs, the money you contribute is done on a pre-tax basis (i.e., the money is contributed before that money is taxed) and then grows on a tax-deferred basis until you withdraw it, at which point you pay taxes on it as if it were income. There are many other pre-tax retirement vehicles available—primarily for businesses—but for our purposes, we'll just focus on these two.

Roth Options

Another type of tax-advantaged retirement account is called a Roth 401(k) or Roth IRA. Unlike the traditional options where you invest pre-tax money, Roth contributions are made using after-tax dollars. Like its traditional counterparts, the Roth options grow on a tax-deferred basis. The primary benefit of a Roth is that your contributions and the earnings on those contributions can be withdrawn completely tax-free, beginning at age 59½ and assuming the account has been open for at least five years. You pay taxes on money before it goes into your Roth IRA, but then all future withdrawals are tax-free. Until recently, 401(k) contributions could only be made on a pre-tax basis. However, more and more employers started adding a Roth option to their plans and now almost 90 percent of all 401(k) plans in the United States offer one, even if this is not advertised much. Changing your contributions from traditional to Roth is likely as simple as checking a box on a website.

If you are like most people who save for retirement, there is a good chance that most of your savings are inside a traditional 401(k) or traditional IRA. If you have been able to build up a nice balance in these plans, you should feel wonderful. These plans became all the rage because of the immediate tax savings contributors received, in addition to the employer match for the lucky ones. Who doesn't like paying less in taxes or getting free money? The problem is that the opportunity is not that clear cut; these traditional options are not so much of a tax savings as much as they are a tax deferral. You are ultimately going to have to pay the tax, just not now.

Which brings us to another big reason why people have always gotten so excited about their pre-tax contributions. If someone is planning for a traditional retirement, the math looks really favorable, because if you are not earning an income when you withdraw the money, you will almost certainly be in a lower tax bracket than you are right now.

Once you decide there is a strong possibility you will be earning income into your 70s or later, however, deferring your tax payments loses a lot of its luster. In fact, there is a good chance you will be in a higher tax bracket in the future because of the combination of your income and the requirement to withdraw money from your pre-tax retirement plans. That's right, I said requirement. It's a tax deferral, remember. Uncle Sam is going to get his money eventually. More to come later in the chapter.

Annuities

Other types of financial instruments that can make sense in the right situation are annuities and variable annuities. As is the case with any investment or insurance product, they can work very well in the right situation and can cause more harm than good when used incorrectly. By integrating annuities into your financial strategy, you can create a steady income stream that supports your lifestyle, long-term goals, and peace of mind.

Annuities are contracts between a person and an insurance company that can guarantee an income amount for either a set period or for the rest of a person's life. While it sounds like insurance, an annuity can operate like a retirement plan and can even give you the opportunity of investing within the annuity.

There are two types of annuities: fixed and variable. Every annuity plan has two phases: an accumulation phase and a payout (annuitization) phase.

The primary difference between fixed and variable annuities is that a fixed annuity provides a guaranteed interest rate during the accumulation phase. It's considered a conservative product, offering modest earnings—usually in line with current interest rates—that are not tied to stock market performance.

A variable annuity includes subaccounts, which are basically mutual funds, and a way for someone to get exposure to the stock market during the accumulation phase. The variable annuity's investment performance will affect the size of the nest egg and how much someone can access later in life.

Both types of annuities are tax-deferred, meaning you are sheltered from current-year taxation on gains, and your tax liability will come when withdrawals start. And just like a traditional 401(k) plan or IRA, you will pay income tax on any gains. Because of this, I would almost never recommend using money that has already been taxed to fund an annuity.

Often, when someone is considering an annuity, they will fund it with pre-tax retirement dollars. You can roll over money from a traditional 401(k) plan or IRA into an annuity without having to realize the tax. Using money to fund an annuity that is already subject to income tax eliminates the biggest reason to avoid using an annuity, in my opinion.

The main reason I suggest annuities as an option to consider is because they allow you to annuitize and guarantee yourself an income stream until you or you and your spouse pass away. You may have concerns about no longer being able to earn an income stream in your 70s or 80s. Or you may have concerns about outliving your money. In either case, setting up an income stream via an annuity is one way to ease those concerns.

The payout phase begins if you choose to annuitize your contract. If you elect this option (it is not always required), you may choose to receive your contract value as a stream of income payments at regular intervals (such as monthly or annually).

You may have choices for how long the payments will last. Under most annuity contracts, you can choose to have your income payments last for a period that you set (such as 20 years) or for an indefinite period (such as your lifetime or the lifetime of your spouse). You may be able to choose between receiving income payments that are fixed in amount or payments that vary based on the performance of mutual fund investment options.

Additionally, it is possible to purchase an immediate annuity. This means that there is no accumulation phase, and you will start receiving income payments shortly after you purchase the annuity.

It is not uncommon for you, as an investor, to have two plans for your money and your life. One plan assumes that things will go the way you are hoping with your health and ability to generate revenue, and could include more frequent and lavish vacations, more dining out, and more charitable donations. You could also have a worst-case-scenario plan where if things don't happen the way you hope they do, you could tighten up your budget. Generating an income stream via an annuity can be a great way to shore up your fallback plan.

Annuities are more complex and more expensive than traditional investment options; however, locking in a guaranteed income for the rest of your life can be worth every penny if it will help you sleep much more easily. However, they are also recommended and used inappropriately, so you need to understand what you're buying. The purchase of most annuities leads to a commission for the seller, which can motivate bad actors with questionable motives (this is also the case with life insurance). Be sure to consult with a financial professional who is well versed in annuities before deciding to use one as part of your plan.

Required Minimum Distributions

Once you reach the year you turn 73 (at the time of writing), federal law requires you to make annual withdrawals from your traditional retirement plans in the form of required minimum distributions (RMDs). You are eligible to take money from these plans without paying an early withdrawal penalty as early as age 59½, but you must take distributions—whether you want to or not—the year you turn 73, with the exception of your first RMD, which can be taken by April 1 of the year after you turn 73.

The required minimum distribution for any year is calculated by using the account balance at the end of the immediately preceding calendar year divided by a distribution period from the IRS's Uniform Lifetime Table. There are two other tables that can be used if the accounts were inherited, or if the sole beneficiary is the owner's spouse who is 10 or more years younger than the owner. For our purposes, we'll focus on the primary Uniform Lifetime Table.

RMDs are subject to federal income tax as ordinary income. They may also be subject to income tax by your state government. When you begin taking your RMDs you will look at the master mortality table to see how long the government expects you to live and use the following equation to determine how much you are required to withdraw: Total Balance across All Accounts ÷ Life Expectancy Factor = Your RMD for that year.

To give you a hypothetical example, let's assume a 75-year-old has $5 million between all her retirement accounts. Her Life Expectancy Factor is 25, which means the government is projecting her to live another 25 years (to age 100). She would be required to take out 1/25th from her total balance, or $200,000 ($5 million ÷ 25), in the first year.

When you add RMDs on top of income from work, it's very likely you won't be in a lower tax bracket later in life. Which also makes it very likely that traditional 401(k)s and IRAs aren't the automatic, no-brainer choices they have been advertised to be for those who will choose to continue working past traditional retirement.

I am not here to tell you that pre-tax retirement contributions are worse than after-tax contributions. It is likely that you should utilize both options, and I want you to have as much information as possible to make the best choices for you.

The more time you have to save money, the more time you have to use the power of compounding interest.

Tax Buckets

The concept of diversifying your assets should be familiar to you, but just in case it isn't, here's a quick refresher. The idea behind diversification is that you have a certain percentage of your investments distributed across different assets, based on your risk tolerance. You might have a set proportion in domestic stocks, international stocks, bonds, real estate, cash, and so on. This diversification can level out the volatility that would come from having all your money in any one of those asset classes.

But here's what most financial professionals don't talk about: diversifying how your money is ultimately going to be *taxed* can be just as important as diversifying between asset classes. Just 3 in 10 Americans believe their retirement plan is tax-efficient, which means the majority will be paying too much in taxes in the future.[1] Properly diversifying for future tax situations involves having three buckets of investments. Given everything we've covered so far, you'll want your money to be distributed across vehicles that are 1) subject to income tax, 2) subject to no tax at all, and 3) subject to capital gains.

To make sure we're on the same page, let's take a moment to define which types of investments could fall into each bucket. I want you to start viewing your long-term investing through the lens of these tax buckets. Here are some examples for each bucket.

Pre-Tax Bucket: traditional 401(k), traditional IRA, SIMPLE IRA, Simplified Employee Pension (a.k.a. SEP IRA), defined benefit plan, cash balance pension plan

Tax-Free Bucket: Roth 401(k), Roth IRA, whole life insurance cash value, municipal bonds

Capital Gains: brokerage accounts, any account that receives after-tax dollars and does not enjoy tax deferral

One of the first things I do with a new client is project into the future how much they will have in each bucket, in both dollars and percentages, relative to the other buckets. It is almost always heavily weighted in favor of the pre-tax bucket. Not only are most of their savings in pre-tax accounts, but this is where most of their projected future savings are headed as well. After they realize they're overweighted in one tax bucket, we prioritize taking steps toward a more balanced outcome in their planning process. This is not because pre-tax contributions are definitively worse than post-tax money. It is because pre-tax money is not so much better that investors should be drastically overweighted in their favor.

If you assume the same initial total investment, the same time frame, the same rate of return, and the same tax bracket, the difference between traditional 401(k)/IRA and Roth 401(k)/IRA contributions is basically a coin flip most of the time.

Pre-tax contributions will usually be best if, in the future, you will earn less income or be in a lower tax bracket. The inverse is true of contributions made into the tax-free bucket. And in keeping with one of the primary themes of this book, who knows what your income and tax bracket are going to be in 20 or 30 years? If you agree that there is some uncertainty involved, you should be creating a plan with more flexibility so you can adjust your plan to what you need now and later.

The last thing you want is to have 80 to 100 percent of your money in pre-tax accounts, especially if you plan to work well into the RMD years. What happens if you save this way and are then greeted with much higher tax rates in the future when you need to make withdrawals? If you take this unbalanced approach, you are unintentionally gambling with the idea that income tax rates are higher now than they will be in the future. Unfortunately, you have no way of knowing that—it's just as likely that income tax rates will be higher in the future than they are now.

While I don't know what will happen any more than you do, I would bet that there is a good chance you will be in a similar or higher tax bracket for the remainder of your life as you are now. Consider the fact that, as of this writing, tax rates in the US are close to historical lows. Even if they are exactly the same 30 years from now, you might be in a higher tax bracket simply as a result of your earning power and career growth, in which case you've already lost. And if taxes go up just 10 percent across the board at every interval, you've truly created a bad deal for yourself.

Let's walk through another example of why this balanced approach can make a big difference for you in the future. Let's say you need $450,000 a year to live on, and the marginal tax rates are the same in the future as they are now. In the US, if you are married and filing jointly, you will pay 24 percent on any income you earn (or take out of pre-tax plans) between $201,050 and $383,900 (as of this writing). Under the current tax structure, any income above $383,900, and up to $487,450, will be taxed not at 24 percent but at 32 percent.

Unfortunately, if you have the majority of your money in pre-tax plans, you have no choice but to take the money out of those accounts when you hit a certain age, which means that to get the $450,000 you need to live on, you are putting yourself into a higher tax bracket, since you'll have to cross over that $383,900 threshold. If you have a more balanced portfolio with some of your funds in accounts that are subject to capital gains tax and some in accounts that are completely tax-free, such as Roth IRAs or cash value from whole life insurance plans, you can withdraw what you need while maintaining a lower marginal tax rate. You could withdraw $383,900 from pre-tax accounts to keep your rate at 24 percent, then withdraw the remaining $66,100 from other tax buckets. You get what you need, while keeping your taxable income lower.

Not all dollars are equal. If you have determined you need to save an amount of money that will eventually provide you with $450,000 annually, the question then becomes, Do you need $450,000 pre-tax or do you need $450,000 post-tax? If you need to accumulate $10 million to be able to live on $450,000 per year, what happens if all of your money is subject to income tax on the way out and tax rates jump by 25 percent when you need the money? (What happens is you will likely run out of money.)

If you find that your projected future buckets are unbalanced, you could consider converting a traditional IRA to a Roth IRA. Regardless of your income, you can convert an existing pre-tax IRA into a Roth by paying the taxes on the balance of the account in the year that you convert it, using your tax rate at the time of the conversion. Obviously, it's important to think about your strategy as far as timing. If you're going to take a sabbatical or you know you'll make less money for a year in the near future for some other reason, that might be a good year to convert to a Roth IRA. As far as taxes go, the amount of money you have in that traditional IRA will be added to your income, which is why you want to avoid converting during a very prosperous year.

Keep in mind that you can't do this with 401(k) plans you have with a current employer. Although there are income limits to Roth IRAs, there is considerable freedom in converting a taxable account to a Roth IRA.

If you want to take on some investments that carry immense upside and immense risk, Roth IRAs are probably the best place to take these types of risks. There's no more famous an example than Peter Thiel, who opened a Roth IRA and accepted initial shares of PayPal through it. Those shares are now worth $5 billion. This means he's got $5 billion in an account that is not subject to any taxes whatsoever on the way out.

How did he do it? When most people think of Roth IRAs, they think of the straightforward type of account with which owners can invest in stocks, mutual funds, bonds, and the like. But Thiel set up a specific kind of Roth IRA—a self-directed IRA—in which you can own assets like real estate and cryptocurrencies, as well as shares of companies. This is where he kept his PayPal shares, allowing them to grow tax-free. There are three or four online companies that allow you to open a Roth account like this one. These accounts are a great option because you won't pay taxes when you buy and sell.

Understanding Risk

Taking on risk and volatility is unavoidable for most people if they want to have a life of enjoyment and freedom. Given the historical performance of the stock market, most people should be (and are) comfortable with exposing themselves to potential short-term dips to their portfolio values in exchange for potentially much higher returns than they can achieve in a savings account. Take, for example, the period between 1927 and 2023, where 94 percent of 10-year periods have been positive. Those who managed to stay in the market through the normal ups and downs have been rewarded for their patience and long-term staying power.[2]

Even though we know that long-term losses haven't happened much in the past, we all understandably struggle when we see our investment retirement accounts drop 35 percent in one year, as was the case in 2008. What people had a hard time embracing was the idea that the loss wasn't locked in unless they sold. If you invest in stocks or mutual funds, you buy shares of those companies or funds. If the value of the stock goes down, you still own the same number of shares. You lose money only if you sell your shares for less than you paid. (This is one of the primary reasons why you should invest money in equities—i.e., stocks and mutual funds—that you will not need for a minimum of 10 years.) As long as you aren't forced into selling because of a short-term need, it's unlikely that you will have to sell at a loss.

Just remember, there are no guarantees when it comes to investing in the stock market and one has to assume the century-plus incredible run of the stock market won't last forever—and yet, as I write this, the S&P 500 just reached (another) all-time high.

Even if the long-term success of the stock market isn't enough to persuade someone to put their long-term eggs into that basket, it is likely they will jump on the bandwagon once they see the alternative. Investing your long-term money into government bonds, certificates of deposit (CDs), and savings accounts—investments that are generally thought of as safe—may come with the likely guarantee that you won't ever see your value decline by double digits, but it will also come with a likely guarantee that you will almost certainly be unexcited about the projected value in 20 years. If a 35-year-old invests $100,000 in the stock market and assumes a 7 percent return over the next 30 years, they will have $761,225 by the time they are 65. If they instead invest this money in a CD that pays 4 percent, they will have only $324,339 at the same age. Investing in stocks isn't a foolproof path to retirement by itself, but not investing in the stock market at all will almost certainly guarantee shortfalls in the plans of many.

This is where you take into consideration the ratio of how much you have invested and how much cash you have on hand. During your earning years, your income covers your current living expenses, and your retirement savings and long-term investments can grow without interruption. As a result, even significant short-term stock market declines won't directly impact your ability to meet your daily needs, even though you'll still feel uncomfortable watching the value of your portfolio fluctuate. Your income buffers you from that volatility.

During their working years, most people can get by with saving about a year's worth of expenses or less in an emergency fund. However, let's say you opt to go the traditional route and retire at 65. If you live to be 95, that's 30 years of not earning an income and needing to live off your investments almost exclusively. This likely means you won't want to be overexposed to the possibility of having to sell your investments during a short-term dip, which means you will need to remove a good portion of your more volatile investments into something more stable like CDs or a money market. Think of it like this: if it makes sense for you to have one year's worth of expenses in an emergency fund while you're earning an income, then five years' worth of expenses is probably the right amount if you are no longer working. Historically, five years has been enough time to allow major declines in the market the opportunity to recover. However, reducing risk also reduces the potential for returns; hopefully, you planned for lower returns on a bigger portion of your net worth before you retired.

Once you decide that traditional retirement at age 65 is not for you, you'll enjoy the likely advantage of exposing yourself to more risk—and potentially greater returns—because your time frame is longer than that of someone who plans to live exclusively off their investments for the rest of their life. Since you will be working longer than your retired counterparts, you won't need to withdraw your funds as quickly. You'll be able to keep more of your money invested because you will need only enough cash to cover one year's worth of living expenses, not five. Being able to extend the time horizon for some of your potentially volatile investments should also help you feel more comfortable with short-term fluctuations in the market, since your income contributes to your bills, and you won't need to rely exclusively, if at all, on the invested money for years.

Compounding Interest and Your New Magic Number

When you decide to work longer and change the age of your retirement, the math works in your favor because you can now leverage compound interest: interest earned on money that was previously earned as interest. The more time you have to save money, the more time you have to use the power of compounding interest. If you continue to work, you'll earn money that will provide an income instead of withdrawing from your savings. At the very least, you won't deplete your savings, and perhaps you'll even continue to contribute to it.

In the previous example, the 35-year-old lets an initial investment of $100,000 build for 30 years and ends up with $761,225 at the age of 65. However, that initial investment in 15 years—that is, by their 50th birthday—is projected to be worth only $275,903. That's quite a significant shift but consider what it would be worth if they worked until the age of 75: allowing the investment to compound for an additional 10 years beyond the traditional retirement age would allow it to grow to $1,497,445—almost a 50 percent increase in

Diversifying how your money is ultimately going to be *taxed* can be just as important as diversifying between asset classes.

exchange for the extra 10 years. Extending the amount of time you have before you retire also gives your investments more time to grow, almost as if you went back in time and saved more in your 20s.

This example highlights the fact that much of the benefit of compounding interest occurs in the later years. The longer you can let it grow, the more it will grow exponentially. The Rule of 72 is a simple way to (very roughly) determine how long an investment will take to double, given a fixed annual rate of interest. By dividing 72 by the annual rate of return, you obtain a rough estimate of how many years it will take for your initial investment to double. If you assume a long-term growth rate of 7 percent, your money will double approximately every 10 years. If you invest $10,000 into an account projected to earn 7 percent, this is how much you will have after a certain number of years:

After 10 years: $20,099
After 20 years: $40,394
After 30 years: $81,184

As you can see, you will slightly more than double your money every 10 years. As you can also see, pulling the money out after 20 years instead of 30 years will cost you quite a bit of money. Most of the money earned will be made in the last years of your investment. The inverse is also true. You can start with the number of years and divide that by 72 to solve for the return you will need to achieve in order to double your money.

Most of the advice around compounding interest is to start as soon as you can. Many articles suggest saving aggressively in your 20s to take advantage of this phenomenon. These articles can be pretty depressing to read if, like me, you weren't thinking about saving for retirement at that age. Even if you were, you were probably earning much less than you are now, and you still have your work cut out for you.

Remember the story of the two Tonys and the vast difference in savings that came from waiting 10 more years to retire? People don't often talk about the fact that we can achieve the same late-year results of saving early by deferring when we take the money out. If your current retirement plan projects you will have $1 million at age 65, you will have $2 million at age 75, according to the Rule of 72. If you earn an income to cover your expenses between age 65 and 75, you won't have to touch that money. Throw in 10 less years of needing to draw down on your investments and this is why the amount of money you are required to save decreases dramatically when you extend your working years.

Not All Returns Are What They Appear to Be

Taking on a higher amount of risk and volatility does have diminishing returns, and not all average annual rates of return are what they appear. Even after you settle on an appropriate risk level, and a corresponding assumed average rate of return, the way in which you achieve this return can greatly impact whether or not you hit your goals.

Before I share an example with you, I'd like to ask you a question: Would you rather put your money in a portfolio that will average 25 percent annually or 5 percent annually?

Before we get into the answer to that question, let's look at a comparison of two hypothetical portfolios to illustrate the nuance of using an average rate of return projection. Let's assume that you put $100,000 into each of the following investments:

Portfolio A: In Year 1, this investment has an incredible year and delivers a 100 percent return. The value of your investment is now $200,000 as a result. Year 2 did not turn out as well. The investment lost 50 percent and now your investment is back down to $100,000 ($200,000 − 50 percent = $100,000).

Portfolio B: In Year 1, this investment does what it was supposed to do and earns 5 percent, bringing your value to $105,000. The investment returns another 5 percent in Year 2, which gives you an ending balance of $110,250.

To recap, Portfolio A averaged 25 percent over two years (100 percent + −50 percent = 50 percent/2 = 25 percent per year) and Portfolio B averaged 5 percent over two years. The correct answer to my initial question is "It depends."

In this example, you did not make a penny over two years with Portfolio A. In fact, you lost money after factoring in inflation. And yet, it's possible and maybe even likely that a fund manager with an annual average of 25 percent would take out a full-page ad in an investment publication touting the portfolio's incredible performance. They wouldn't be lying.

Even though Portfolio B only averaged 5 percent annually, you would have made over 10 percent cumulatively by the end of the second year. In this example, Portfolio B smoked Portfolio A.

Here's another hypothetical to consider: If you invest $100,000 into a portfolio that loses 50 percent in Year 1, you will need to earn much more than 50 percent in Year 2 to get back to even—100 percent to be exact. If you earn 50 percent in Year 2, your $50,000 will only grow to $75,000. This $25,000 loss in value will be a tough pill for many to swallow considering the investment's average annual return over this period is 0 percent, or flat.

I share these examples with you to highlight the importance of not relying on a linear annual return for planning purposes when evaluating the amount of risk versus growth in your investments over a long period of time. Prioritize investments that minimize volatility over those that could experience wild swings.

Planning for a fulfilling and financially stable life requires looking at more than just your balance sheet. By taking a holistic view across areas like tax diversification, investment risk, coordinating distributions, and the option to work longer, you set yourself up for long-term success. Having your savings strategically distributed across pre-tax, post-tax, and tax-free accounts will help minimize your tax liability in retirement. Continuing to properly invest based on your timeline and risk tolerance, rather than becoming overly conservative, will allow your money the potential to grow. Being thoughtful about which accounts you pull from and when can help reduce your tax burden. And working just a few years longer leverages compound growth and delays withdrawals.

While each area on its own is impactful, coordinating efforts across these pillars creates a plan that can stand the test of time. With the right pillars firmly in place, you can feel confident in your outlook for your later years—as well as right now.

{ 10 }

Investing in You

AFTER YEARS of working with clients, I've noticed that most people don't actually want a lot of money for the sake of having a lot of money. Most people want the feeling they think having a lot of money—and the stuff it buys—will give them. But as soon as we buy into the belief that we'll be happier or more fulfilled when we have more money or when we retire, we're making retirement or money a prerequisite to happiness. We're essentially saying that we need those things to feel good, or we can't be happy before we have them... and that we're willing to wait decades to feel satisfied or content.

In recent chapters, I've talked a lot about smart financial planning and how time and compounding interest work in your favor and yield tremendous results when you use them well. But compound interest does not just apply to the realm of personal finance. The same principle of compounding that applies to money can also apply to other areas of life, like health and relationships. Both also benefit from small, incremental deposits over long periods of time.

I've heard a lot of stories of people who were focused on making sure they saved early and often to leverage compound interest in their retirement portfolios, and yet completely failed to leverage compound interest in other areas of their lives. Whether they were on track or behind the eight ball, so many of them worried to the point that they worked long hours and sacrificed more of their time to catch up or keep pace with where they thought they were supposed to be. Oftentimes, this effort came at the expense of their health and relationships.

If you're working hard to save money to retire by a certain age, some of the sacrifices you're likely making are less sleep, less time at the gym, less fun, and less time with your friends and family in exchange for more time at your desk. When you sacrifice time for work, you typically don't have the time to make healthy meals for yourself or spend with the people you love, and you probably aren't getting to bed early. If that's the case, you're not going to get the compounding benefits of those small, daily decisions.

Throughout this book, I've been dismantling the core tenet of traditional retirement: that you should forgo living a life you love right now for the sake of living a life you dream of in the distant future. By now, you've seen that the traditional concept of retirement may have put you on autopilot in other areas as well. Now that you realize that rigid approach is probably not what you want for yourself, I invite you to consider what other parts of your life may also be on autopilot—like your health and relationships.

A year of well-being today is more valuable than a year 20 years from now. In most cases, a year lived fully in the present is better than a year lived 20 years in the future, regardless of age, in terms of what we can do with that time. If we want to spend more of our time and money on the people and priorities that matter right now, we need to make different choices about how we spend our days. When we make the choice to lengthen our working years, we should not feel the same financial burden to aggressively save and can feel better about small indulgences—a bit more time sleeping, meditating, exercising, socializing—that grant us joy and fulfillment in the present moment. If we invest in the right practices and habits, we won't just feel better in an hour or a week. We will lay a foundation to improve our lives in the future as well.

In this section, we're going to flip the script and talk about how, when it comes to your health and relationships, incremental changes really do pay off over time. It's like compounding interest, only harder to track.

Your Relationship with Yourself

While I was writing this book, quite a few things happened: we survived a pandemic, the way I worked in my business changed, and my father and beloved dog, Bodie, died, just to name a few. One of the biggest changes for me was moving out of our condo in Washington, DC, and into a much larger, single-family home in the suburbs. One day I was sitting on my back porch reminiscing about the early days of my career when I was working 80 hours per week, and I spent much of my time making a hundred cold calls per day. The reason I had worked so hard back then—and for the following 20 years—is because I wanted what I have now. I wanted a beautiful family and a dream home for us to live in. It occurred to me in that moment on the porch that the younger version of me would be confused as to why I was not happier. Don't get me wrong, I was not unhappy. However, I did not feel as good as I had imagined I would. If I had everything I wanted, why did I always feel so unsettled in my body?

For the first time in a long time, I decided to slow down. I reminded myself that because I don't ever plan to retire, I could reduce my work hours to spend more time with my family and explore the source of all my anxiety.

For many years I thought self-care meant going to the gym five times a week and taking 50 supplements every morning, but I was also consuming 15 to 20 servings of nicotine daily, along with a glass or two of wine every night—all in the name of subconsciously avoiding my emotions. One day I caught myself saying, "I need nicotine to focus," which led me to wonder where else I felt like I needed something in order to feel a certain way. Some other examples for me included "I need a glass of wine to relax," and "I need a pint of ice cream because I had a tough day." I realized that by saying I needed something to feel a certain way, I was also saying I couldn't feel the way I wanted to feel without the crutch.

One day, I decided to quit all my coping mechanisms and addictions and see what would happen. Unsurprisingly, I didn't feel that good. By the way, I don't recommend quitting everything all at once. I made it far harder than it had to be. If you are like me and have multiple coping mechanisms you rely on to avoid experiencing unpleasant feelings and emotions, you should take it slow. Cold turkey is a lot to ask of anybody.

Over many months, I committed to building practices that would help me stop avoiding these feelings and emotions. I prioritized sleep, started a daily meditation practice after trying and failing for years, and practiced other forms of reflection such as walks and journaling. Because of my change of pace, my relationship with myself started to change, and I noticed certain habits and patterns that I'd developed over the course of my life.

One day during meditation, I was presented with a series of flashbacks from my childhood. I was bullied a lot growing up. One time in seventh grade, an entire classroom of kids chanted, "Who do we hate? We hate Derek!" I frequently got into trouble due to my ADHD and my inability to sit still and behave, which caused my grades to suffer—teachers often told me that I would not be successful. Most of the girls I tried to date rejected me, and I was teased that I would never have a girlfriend.

My life became one big response to all my haters. Subconsciously, I was operating with an attitude that said, "Oh, you don't think I can [fill in the blank]? Watch me!" Don't get me wrong; this motivation led to many wonderful things in my life. I have two successful businesses, more friends than most adults, and I am married to the most incredible woman on the planet!

Slowing down helped me see that my life evolved largely around proving others wrong. I'm grateful for what it gave me, but I got to a place in life where external validation ceased to provide meaning. I had succeeded on other people's terms rather than my own. Even though I no longer felt I had to prove myself to anyone, that energy still persisted within me. If my body could speak, every morning it would have said, "Who are we going to prove something to today?" To deal with all this energy, I used a lot of substances and techniques to suppress my trauma in order keep the train going.

I believe that had I not figured this out, it would have manifested itself in health issues later in life. I was forming tension in my body as a result of childhood trauma and self-medicating so that I didn't have to be bothered by it. I can only imagine how much easier it will be on my organs and central nervous system not to spend the rest of my life working hard to overcome all the stress and uncomfortable emotions I created.

By hitting pause, I could see I was living life on someone else's terms rather than my own. Once I did the work to unwind this fuel that I no longer needed—and to be honest, I am still working on it—I unlocked a new level of creativity and fulfillment. I was able to see new paths for my time and energy, and I found the motivation to finish this book.

I share this to illustrate how easy it is to operate on autopilot unless we consciously create space for self-reflection. This kind of reflection is accessible to anyone—I have many friends who have confronted lifelong patterns resulting from never making their parents happy, being the less successful sibling, or not feeling worthy of love.

The main theme here is that we have to invest in ourselves, our whole selves—physically, emotionally, mentally, and spiritually. And investing in ourselves looks different for everyone. It's less about money and more about making time to prioritize practices that nurture you holistically. I hope that by sharing my personal story you will be inspired to create more space in your life to explore patterns and habits that may be holding you back from your true potential.

Sleep

Pulling a late night or an all-nighter here and there is fairly harmless. It certainly feels harmless in our 20s and 30s. But more and more studies are revealing the effects of shorting yourself on sleep over an extended period. These studies strengthen our understanding of already known and suspected relationships between inadequate sleep and hypertension, impaired immunity, cardiovascular disease, diabetes, mood disorders, and neurodegenerative diseases and dementia, and even loneliness.[1] Even the kind of sleep we get is important: one study found REM sleep to be the strongest predictor of longevity. It showed a linear relationship between the amount of REM sleep and lifespan, with a 5 percent reduction in REM sleep associated with a 13 percent increased risk of mortality.[2] Whatever study you look at, it's clear that you can't ignore sleep in favor of work for 30 years, then suddenly decide to get eight hours of sleep per night and expect everything to be fine.

Getting great sleep will help you live longer, but the main reason I want you to sleep well is because of how much it will change your life *right now*. If you don't wake up feeling refreshed and energized in the morning, it's likely that you are not getting the right amount or right quality of sleep. My sleep really improved when I eliminated alcohol and food close to bedtime, refined my diet, and retrained my body to sleep with my mouth closed, but the improvements really began when I started tracking the quality of my sleep with wearable technology. You could consider investing in something like an Oura Ring or a WHOOP wristband. I use the Oura Ring to track my sleep, and it's helped me understand my sleep cycles, the optimal time to go to bed, and what I should (and shouldn't) eat or drink before bed. In 2020, my average sleep score was 69 out of 100—a pretty poor number. In 2021, it was 77; in 2022, it was 82; and in 2023, it was 85. These improvements have made an incredible difference in how I feel every day. All the effort is worth it when I wake up feeling great. The quality of my decisions and choices across the board simply gets much better with consistent, high-quality sleep.

There are plenty of books about sleep optimization, and I didn't read any of them. I just implemented small habit changes that worked for me. You don't necessarily need to follow a prescribed program—start with some incremental changes that address areas you think could be improved. My first experiments included skipping my usual glass of wine every night, not eating anything within three hours of bedtime, and going to bed earlier. If you know you wake up because you're hot, start by adjusting the temperature in your room. If you snore, look into ways to address that. If you wake up feeling groggy, go to bed 15 minutes earlier every day until you hit the point where you're getting enough sleep. Just be patient and pay attention to the compound benefits over time.

If you're convinced in the back of your mind that you need to keep working hard to build your nest egg, or working hard to build your business, you might also think that going to bed at an earlier time is going to conflict with those plans. It might seem that way at first glance, but getting better sleep gives you more energy. I can attest to this personally: sleeping better has made me a more productive business owner with far more energy and drive to get work done. I show up better in every single area of my life when I sleep well.

Sleep is really important. The quality of your sleep directly affects your longevity and your overall health, as well as your ability to withstand illness. If your sleep isn't good, you're probably not enjoying the best quality of life you could be experiencing right now. And you're certainly not setting yourself up in the future to have the kind of quality of life possible for somebody getting good quality sleep every night.

Exercise

In a conversation between Dr. Peter Attia, the longevity expert mentioned earlier in the book, and Dr. Michael Joyner, the two doctors discuss how cardiovascular fitness can add somewhere between three to five years to your lifespan... and six to eight years to your health span.[3] The best part is that it doesn't require much investment to get that kind of upside. If you exercised four hours per week, every week, for 50 years, that would be 10,000 hours of exercise. That's barely over one year of time cumulatively. In exchange for that year of time, you would likely get six to eight additional years of health.[4] Another way to think of it is that for every hour you spend exercising, you might gain six to eight hours of healthy life.

But if you take the easy way out, it's going to sneak up on you.

You may not like going to the gym, and you may not notice a change for two or three months after routinely exercising, but you will definitely feel the effects over a period of years. Maybe more importantly, you will certainly feel the effects of choosing *not* to exercise. You can't ignore working out for significant periods of time and then expect to be able to pick it up when you have "more time to dedicate" to it.

People say they exercise for "sanity and vanity." It may take a little while for your physique to change, but you should feel the mental effects almost immediately. If you already work out regularly, you know what I am talking about. If you currently do not exercise much, adding this to the ways you invest in yourself will produce massive ripple effects on your life. Over the years I have consistently lifted weights; I have also sprinkled in CrossFit, yoga, Pilates, and jujitsu, to name a few. My goal is to one day be a perennial champion in the faux Grandparent Olympics, which is why I also make time for stretching and mobility work.

There are plenty of options for all of us to consider, and I encourage you to have fun finding what works for you, especially if you've been putting it off because you needed the extra time to work and save more.

Having More Fun

Take a moment and consider these questions: When was the last time you had fun? What exactly did you do for fun, and how often do you have fun like that?

Now if you were to share your current idea of fun with the past version of you that valued fun the most, whether it was your childhood self, your teenage self, or some other version of you that loved having a good time, would they be impressed? Would they think you're really having a good time, or would that version be in utter disbelief that your life is this boring?

If you're like most folks in midlife, your answers might be a tad disappointing, at least to a younger version of yourself. You might not even remember the last time you had fun, and you might tell yourself this is normal for a middle-aged person.

Based on a rough, informal survey of my friends, I'm confident there is a strong chance you feel inadequate in this department right now. It's even possible you feel triggered by the topic. Take a deep breath and please bear in mind that my only objective right now is to encourage and support you to enjoy this one life you have just a little bit more. I believe we are in the midst of a fun recession, and I want to help the world remember our natural, playful disposition. We are going to come up with a plan to bring some fun back into your life, because you deserve to have a lot of fun, in a variety of ways, on a regular basis. Life can be hard. Work and relationships and parenting can be hard. If we have to experience the hard knocks of life sometimes, shouldn't we experience pure bliss too?

A friend recently saw me post about my concert-going and said it was nice to see one of her friends having so much fun. I told her I believe most adults aren't treating themselves to a good time often enough. She agreed and mentioned she was having fun and being playful with a client earlier that day. I said that's great, but I am referring to the type of fun that leaves you exhilarated and needing to recover. The kind of fun where your endorphins spike and you know you've had a very good time.

When I say fun, I'm talking about those moments where you forget yourself and become a part of something bigger than you, something that can only exist in that moment. It's like a flow state—your heart races and you don't think about

I believe we are in the midst of a fun recession.

anything but what you're experiencing. It's even better when you are in a shared energetic space with other people who are feeling the same thing. It's the feeling of "being free" and letting loose.

It's unfortunate that I feel I have to dedicate a few paragraphs to encouraging most of you to have more fun in your life, but alas, our current societal norms are quite discouraging. Part of our struggle with fun is our underlying belief that fun wastes time. Our collective work ethic gets in the way; we've focused so much on productivity that if we spend time on an activity that doesn't have a tangible ROI, we don't see the value in it. Studies have shown that the more participants believed that fun and leisure were wasteful, the less they enjoyed a given activity.[5] That mindset seemed to affect their well-being too. The more they thought of fun as a waste of time, the higher the degree of their depression, stress, and anxiety. Not surprisingly, their reported levels of happiness were also lower. The inverse was true too; viewing fun and leisure as beneficial rather than wasteful led to lower stress levels and improved mental health.

What sucks about this state of affairs is that when we miss out on fun and play, we miss out on all of the incredible benefits they bring. Having fun can help balance hormone levels, reduce stress, and improve mood and energy levels.[6] Play and fun contribute to brain and emotional health by creating new neural pathways, improving our social interactions, and supporting our problem-solving skills.[7] Fun also fosters creativity and helps us develop strategies to adapt to new situations, which are crucial for our development and growth.[8]

Should you need any more convincing, happiness and fun lead to increased productivity. A study published in 2023 found that happiness boosted productivity by leaps and bounds. Each additional unit of happiness (on a scale of 1 to 10) amounted to a 12 percent increase in productivity.[9]

Think about how often you currently have fun and whether you plan for it. Fun doesn't happen by accident.

What have you done in the past that brought you joy?

Think about what exactly made those experiences fun. It might be true that the way you have fun in your 20s and 30s is a little different than the way you want to (or can) have fun when you're 40 or older, but the goal here isn't to recreate memories from the past. Instead, I want you to think about those gold-star moments that you'll never forget and what made them so fantastic. Who were you with? What did you do? If you loved going to bars when you were younger but, like most of us, have no desire to drink like you did then, think about the other elements you enjoyed. Did you like spending time with friends? Did you love to dance? Did you like finding new spots in your city and meeting new people? Did you like the spontaneity of the night's events, and do you miss the feeling that anything could happen?

There are dozens of ways to recreate that feeling that don't have to involve bars and sticky bathroom floors covered in who-knows-what. The point is to deconstruct the fun you had and think about how you can incorporate those elements into your life now.

That's why I love live music so much. I know this is subjective and everyone has a different definition of fun, but in my opinion, live music is the best catalyst for having a blast. I strongly believe the number one thing you can do to improve the amount of fun you're having is to go see live music. It could be a concert or a DJ set. It doesn't have to be expensive: the average ticket price of the last five shows I saw was $27.

Also, please don't confuse what's fun for you as a family with what's fun for you as an individual. You and your kids might enjoy hiking or watching superhero movies together because that works well in a family setting, but that doesn't mean you shouldn't pursue your version of fun. Taking my boys to see Pearl Jam is one type of great fun. Seeing Pearl Jam in a standing-room-only general admission pit with my wife and friends is a few notches higher. Maybe you and your partner like to do things your kids find boring. Make time to go out without them. Maybe you and your friends find traveling to old bookstores fascinating, but your partner would rather die than do that. Go have your version of fun. I promise you'll be better off for it.

If you're stuck on ideas, I'm always a proponent of live music. Go find a show in your city next week and take your friends or your partner. There is a great app called Bandsintown that will sync with your Spotify account and curate a list of upcoming shows in your area based on your listening history.

Stand-up comedy is right up there with live music in its ability to allow you to forget about time while sharing a high vibration with a large group of people. Comedy is an easy entry into fun because you don't need to know the comedian before you go.

Whatever it is you do, make sure it has a low barrier to entry. If you haven't run for exercise in years, you wouldn't start out tomorrow by running 10 miles. Don't make the first attempt at having more fun financially or logistically difficult, like traveling to a far-off location or going to an event that costs half your mortgage payments for a year. Start small. Try new things at the local level that have little to no risk.

Finally, don't make fun a once-a-year thing. I know guys who go on a golf trip once a year with their buddies and have fun for 3 days out of every 365 days. That is not enough. A regular cadence of events or activities that fill you up is far more important and beneficial than a blowout trip once a year.

So what's your definition of fun, and does it need an upgrade? When was the last time you thought about what it meant to have fun?

Lifelong Learning

We've never had more access to education. Right now, there are thousands of Ivy League classes available for free online. We have access to books from all over the world, apps like MasterClass and Udemy, and no shortage of other ways to learn. There are volunteer opportunities with amazing organizations that are always looking for help from people willing to learn and provide support. I also recommend attending conferences and joining professional communities that could contribute to your growth as an individual and as a professional. There is no excuse not to keep learning and growing, no matter your age. If you're in your 50s and 60s and ready to turn toward something else, it's easier than ever to invest the time and money into learning new skills or improving existing ones. And you might even meet some interesting people along the way.

If we want to spend more time and money on what's truly important, let's make that a lifestyle and way of being. Now that retirement isn't a deadline forcing aggressive savings, we can feel good about small indulgences—a bit more sleep, meditation, exercise, and other practices that recharge us. That means making different choices day to day, given this new perspective on working longer. The goal is to achieve a high quality of life all along the journey, not to delay the payoff. Don't put off feeling good until some future date. A year of fulfillment now is worth more than a year of fulfillment in some hypothetical future.

We need to go beyond thinking about how we want to retire; we have to ask ourselves whom we want to retire *with*.

Your Primary Relationship

Those who plan to traditionally retire and travel the world with their partners but haven't been available to them over the years face the stark reality that they won't have a partner to retire with by the time they're ready. I know someone in his 70s who has multiple successful businesses. He told me his wife doesn't think he spends enough time with her, and I immediately replied, "Because you don't." He's spent so much time building up his wealth and success that now he goes home only to be reminded of what a terrible husband he's been, which doesn't feel very good. Why should someone like him spend more time with people who resent him for his absence when he can go to the office and feel a sense of accomplishment, empowerment, and control?

A good segment of the population believes their work is their life and identity. Some of these people are really happy, but I would argue that most are not. Too many people I know double down on work because that's where they feel the most valued, the most significant. This creates a feedback loop where the more time they spend at work, the more they're applauded for it and the better they feel. But when they return to their family and friends, and those relationships don't come as easily, they get a different kind of feedback that doesn't feel as good—which only drives them to want to return to work. Would you rather spend more time around people who think you're amazing or people who are disappointed in how you've shown up for them over time?

It might seem a lot easier to play where it's safe, but if your relationship with your partner is important to you (and it should be!), then you have to figure out a way to work on it. Going back to the person I know, we may think the issue is simply his relationship with his wife, but his relationship with his work also affects this dynamic. He's driven by motivations he's not even aware of. Like most of us, he's probably built up attachments that are hard to break—attachments to feeling good, to the adrenaline high of success and impact. People love being in control, and he probably feels more control over his work life than he does over his home life. But his home life won't improve until he takes the time and builds up the courage to let go of control and actually show up for the people in his life—and does the repair work needed for those relationships to thrive.

My wife and I have been going to see a therapist once a week, for an hour at a time, for 18 years. We started going out of necessity, but we continued to go because we recognized that even though our relationship improved and has mostly been in a great place ever since, it's important for us to carve out this dedicated time to talk about our concerns and emotions. If we don't, we know that our relationship will suffer and, over time, will start to deteriorate. We both feel so much security because we set this hour aside specifically to talk about *us*. That incremental effort builds up, and we can move through problems relatively smoothly because we know we'll make the time to do it.

The one-hour time commitment every week is a deposit in our relationship that has built up over time and continues to pay off. At $250 an hour, we have invested over $250,000 into our relationship via therapy alone. That money would have been worth a few million dollars had I been investing it along the way, and I'll pass on calculating what it would have been worth 20 years from now. However, the ROI on being in a thriving relationship and being more in love with my wife today than I was when we got married is priceless.

I am quite certain that I have generated a lot more money over the past 20 years because I am in a fulfilling relationship with my best friend who loves and supports me... more than I would have had I been in a mediocre relationship (or divorced). If you have let your primary relationship get off track, I would invest the time, energy, and money necessary to rekindle the flame if possible. Or, find a way out. As the well-known proverb goes, "The best time to plant a tree was 20 years ago. The second best time is today." Regular date nights or long weekends away can help foster and maintain that sense of connection with your partner. Over the years, Melanie and I have been diligent about planning time together, and every time life gets in the way, our relationship suffers. Our connection grows and we're both happier when we make it a priority.

Unlike someone who is planning for a traditional retirement where they will travel the world with their spouse—while mostly ignoring them until they get there—you can start planning dates and experiences with your spouse right now as part of your plan to work beyond the typical retirement age. You can feel much better about taking time away and spending the money on these experiences now because you'll be investing in the relationship that's most important to you.

Friendship and Connection

Wendy Suzuki is an award-winning professor of neural science and psychology. She studies the effects of physical activity and meditation on the brain. She says that the number one predictor of a long life is the number of positive social connections you have.[10] Andrew Huberman, popular neuroscientist and podcaster, says there are five things everyone should do every day: get good sleep, get sunlight within

10 minutes of waking up, move, eat healthy food, and build connection into your day.[11]

There is countless evidence that strong friendships and connections are vital to our well-being. Studies show that people who experience social isolation face a 50 percent greater chance of premature death than those who have healthy social connections.[12] Researchers have found that the stress of loneliness can lead to weakened immunity, making people more vulnerable to disease.[13] Even the perception of loneliness has been tied to a 29 percent increase in the risk of heart disease and a 32 percent increase in the risk of stroke.[14]

We're not quite sure why health suffers so much when we're socially isolated, but some theories provide potential explanations. For example, research suggests that people who are alone more often may be more likely to engage in unhealthy behaviors like smoking, alcohol overuse, or overeating that leads to weight gain. Another theory is that loneliness can trigger physical changes by increasing the activity of the sympathetic nervous system, which controls the body's stress response. This heightened stress response over time then contributes to poorer health.[15]

Given all this, we need to go beyond thinking about how we want to retire; we have to ask ourselves whom we want to retire *with*. The more time we spend with the people we love, the more connected we'll be later in life.

Early on, I saw the importance and value of solid connections in life. A lot of folks gloss over this and say they've got 10 friends, or their group of friends from college, and they text each other from time to time. They think they're checking the box of friendship, but they don't realize that there's so much more to it than that. Sure, texting your friends once in a while is better than nothing, but you wouldn't take vitamin D once a month and expect it to do anything for you. Why would you expect that of anything else?

I knew I was doing something right when it came to friendships on the day of my dad's funeral. The sheer number of people who showed up to support me took my breath away. It was an hour's drive for most of my friends, and for them to take that time for me made me feel loved and cared for. When our dog Bodie passed away, over 30 people came to say goodbye and grieve with us. Those were stop-me-in-my-tracks moments that showed me the value of friendship.

To be clear, I never had a plan or a strategy about how to build and maintain relationships. And it didn't come naturally. My parents didn't really model friendships for me. Neither of them had close friends to whom they could really open up. They were high school sweethearts who went all in on their kids but didn't really build relationships outside of their family, although my dad liked to play cards with a loose group of friends and my mom spent a lot of time talking to her mother and siblings.

In my early years, I often felt rejected as a kid. I never seemed to fit in. It didn't take long for me to get really good at figuring out what to say to get people to like me. It took me a long time to let go of my people-pleasing tendencies as an adult, but they got me by as a kid. For years as an adult, I bent over backward to do things for others, no matter how I felt about it. Now I let things go. If you people-please over and over again, you lose a little of your soul. I've gotten good at saying yes only to those things that are a "hell yes."

In *The Myth of Normal*, Dr. Gabor Maté has an entire chapter on the intersection between attachment and authenticity. He describes this constant tug and pull between our need for attachment to other people and our need to live our truth. If you want to be completely authentic all the time, then you'll probably have fewer people in your life. If you're going out of your way to make other people happy all the time, they'll hang out with you, but you'll be miserable. You've got to turn the knobs and levers in the right way so you have the right mix of being you and having meaningful friendships and connections with the people you love.

Right now, start by strengthening your present relationships with the people you like. Stay in touch with existing friends, family, and loved ones by creating shared experiences and memories. Check in with them on a regular basis—this doesn't mean you have to check in with hundreds of people every day, but develop a cadence and a way of thinking about your connections that helps you stay in touch with the people you value. Be sure to show the people you care about that you're grateful for their continued presence in your life.

As you get older, don't take the approach that most people do—don't stop building your connections. Continue to meet new people. Go to community events, seek out new experiences through clubs and organizations, and volunteer for a cause you care about. Meeting new people should be a part of your lifestyle, no matter where you are in life. Going out of your way to put yourself into new settings is a great way to keep life interesting and keep your network fresh and growing.

You'll Like Giving

Most people wait until later in life to start giving their money away to charities and organizations that matter to them. They wait because they don't want to give away money they may need one day, which makes sense if they stop working and realize they may not have properly planned for all the potentially unexpected changes and expenses that come with growing older. One significant downside of this approach is deferring the happiness that comes with giving to others.

I believe we do everything we do because we think it will make us feel better. This may surprise you, but I do not give for purely altruistic reasons. I love helping people and organizations in need and I love how good it makes me feel to contribute. I am not going to deprive myself of the increased endorphins because society has told me my donations aren't as meaningful if I am making them for selfish reasons.

There are many studies that highlight how giving increases when people choose to spend money on others rather than themselves, especially when they choose how much and to whom the money is given (as opposed to feeling compelled to give).[16] Whether we feel we have a little or a lot to give away, how we choose to spend the money matters more to our happiness. The same is true of the way we spend our time.

My friend John Ruhlin embodied giving and generosity unlike anyone I've ever met. We often worked with John and his company Gift·ology to give gifts to many of our clients and friends over the years. Unfortunately, he lost his life unexpectedly, but his legacy in giving lives on with his company and in the memories of those he touched with his generous spirit.

Since you know that you will earn an income for longer than you previously thought, I want you to benefit from the happiness your giving will generate right now. If you are not currently donating to charity, I encourage you to start small. It could be your church or alma mater. I Like Giving is a great organization that can help you get in the giving mood by providing a lot of great resources.

Everything we've discussed in this chapter serves to increase your health span, as opposed to your lifespan. There's no point in saving for retirement and working on your longevity if your health and relationships suffer along the way. Taking better care of yourself now yields incremental rewards over time; one good decision often leads to another. You don't always have to wait months or years to see the benefits either. Just like you want to experience the benefits of giving now, making small tweaks and changes to the way you live today can help you feel better right away.

Conclusion

IF YOU DO NOT feel fulfilled right now, I do not believe you will feel fulfilled in the future just because you have a lot of money and no longer have to work.

We know this about life: far more value comes from enjoying the journey and learning along the way than reaching the destination. And yet, too many of us have bought into the idea that we can only be happy "someday," when we retire or stop working. Traditional retirement is often seen as the pot of gold at the end of the rainbow—a time when you can finally relax, travel, pursue hobbies, and do all the things you postponed during your working years. This constant messaging distracts us from exploring how we can be happy and free right now. Far too many of us have been duped into believing that we can't enjoy life while we work toward achieving our financial goals.

Our belief that achieving a goal will bring us happiness drives us to pursue it. But when we focus solely on the result, we lose sight of the feelings we hope it will bring. If we were to take a step back, we would realize that we rarely need our object of fixation to feel the way we want to feel. Think back to the last time you believed an experience, a purchase, or a major change would change how you feel in a meaningful way. Maybe you thought buying a new car would provide a lasting feeling of excitement. Or getting a raise would be the catalyst to finally turn your life around. In all likelihood, once you got what you wanted, it lost its power and didn't produce the lasting feeling you were hoping for.

People have spent their entire lives believing that retiring with a certain amount of money will finally make them happy. So many of them reach the promised land and don't feel the way they expected to feel. I wrote this book to prevent you from suffering this fate.

I hope *Let's Retire Retirement* has convinced you that you don't have to live life this way, that you can choose to create a life you love now instead of putting it off. You can start feeling better now instead of sacrificing your happiness for some distant future.

We've explored the paradigm shift away from the traditional concept of retirement toward a more fulfilling, flexible approach to life and work. We no longer have to practice extreme forms of delayed gratification for a future that may be very different from the one we're expecting. We can redefine success and happiness in terms that are meaningful to us now. Fulfillment comes from engaging in work that resonates with our values and passions, allowing us to live fully at every stage of life, not just after we've stopped working. By committing to working longer—not out of necessity, but out of a desire to continue growing and contributing—we open ourselves up to a wealth of opportunities for personal and financial growth.

This journey toward a reimagined future emphasizes the importance of being present in our daily lives. It teaches us to appreciate the beauty of the moment, the satisfaction of

People have spent their entire lives believing that retiring with a certain amount of money will finally make them happy.

hard work, and the joy of connection with others. These are the true treasures of life, far surpassing any material wealth we might build along the way.

You can take the first steps toward redefining life on your terms by building a solid financial plan that reflects your goals and desires, not just the arbitrary benchmarks society sets for us. Your plan should serve as a flexible framework, adaptable to life's inevitable changes and designed to support the life you dream of living, both now and in the future. I hope I've helped you identify what truly matters to you so you can allocate your resources in a way that brings joy to your life now and later. By doing so, you're not just planning for a solid financial future; you're sculpting a life rich with purpose and joy, tailored to your deepest aspirations.

Happiness is not found in accomplishment. It's not found by acquiring stuff. It's not in reaching a destination. It's in the relationships with the people who are most important to you. It's in a healthy body and a calm nervous system. It's in being able to be present during the journey. It's in the great experiences you have along the way—the ones that will become stories you can tell your grandkids.

I want you to enjoy your life in 20 years' time and I want you to enjoy your life even more right now. And I know you will likely enjoy your life more in 20 years if you start enjoying it more tomorrow. Let this book inspire you to break free from outdated notions of success and happiness tied solely to retirement. Don't wait for "someday" to live fully—make the choice today to create a life so fulfilling that the idea of retiring from it seems unimaginable.

Start today by making choices that align with your deepest desires and values. You have some amazing gifts to share with the world, and we don't want to have to wait any longer to experience the best version of you!

Acknowledgments

SARA STIBITZ, you were the ultimate writing partner. Your ability to take my scatterbrained ideas and writing and turn them into cohesive and easy-to-read words on paper is truly remarkable. Anyone who loves this book should send you a gift because it would not have been nearly as good without you. Thank you for coming out of "retirement" to help me finish this book.

Trena White and the team at Page Two, thank you so much for your support. Trena, your encouraging words and excitement about this project meant more to me than you know. Your support came at a time when I was seriously considering whether to continue with this book or not, and your belief in the project gave me the nudge to keep moving forward.

Scott Steedman, Adrineh Der-Boghossian, and Carmen Ho, thank you for your insightful edits, guidance, and support, all of which helped make this book a better experience for the reader.

Joe DeNoyior, you've been a longtime friend and business partner in the wealth management world, and your selfless attitude and generous spirit provided me with many opportunities to succeed throughout my career. Thank you for your partnership, friendship, and support.

Mark Jensen, my longtime friend and right-hand man, and Jay Sanford, my chief investment officer, I appreciate our friendship and teamwork over the years. Without you two and the rest of the team, I wouldn't have had the ability to focus on the bigger picture and write this book. Thank you for everything you do.

Joe Mechlinski, thanks for cheering me on during the entire writing process, especially during the moments when it seemed like a better idea to throw in the towel. Thanks for sending me articles, stats, and encouragement in support of this idea. One of my favorite parts of our relationship is how much we support and encourage each other in our goals.

Joey Coleman, thanks for writing two excellent books and learning a ton about the process along the way so you could generously share your incredible wisdom with me (and so many others) to make this book better. I am super grateful for your friendship and support!

Scott Thompson, thanks for always believing in me and supporting me when I felt lost during this process. We've been on similar paths and having you there to walk beside me has been a gift. Thank you for always being there for me, and for pushing me to improve.

Jere Simpson and Borzou Azabdaftari, thanks for your friendship and advice along the way, especially around the cover design.

Dave Schmidgall, my former pastor and good friend, thank you for being so supportive of me. You've been one of my greatest spiritual role models, and you've helped me cultivate a deeper relationship with God. Thank you for supporting my family and me through our various ups and downs.

Christian Genetski, I imagine few people get to experience the type of friendship we've had for over 20 years. Your consistency, reliability, and unconditional support have provided an incredible home base for me. I am super grateful for the way you show up in the world and the way you have shown up for me.

Serena Porter, we use the term "chosen family" a lot in our home and you are the first person that comes to mind when I think about that term. I would not have had the success I enjoyed in my wealth management practice without your support, and that pales in comparison to the way you have loved and cared for my boys over the years.

To all of the people who have pushed me creatively with encouragement and their work as I wrote this book, including Garrett Gunderson, Yanik Silver, Jayson Gaignard, Marcus Sheridan, Oren Harris, Ronsley Vaz, Dan Martell, Rob Weinhold, Jesse Elder, Mark Batterson, Zvi Band, Philip McKernan, Aaron Copeland, Kirk Drake, Eli Facenda, Barry Glassman, Paul Gustavson, Will Hamilton, Nate Hurd, Sally Hogshead, Tracey Ivanyshyn, Joe Fuld, Laura Gassner Otting, Re Perez, and Chris Yoko.

To all of my wonderful chosen family and friends who have supported me along this journey including Patrice Webb, Jayson and LaShondra Mercurius, Ron and Nicole Novak, Sherry Walling, Trey Whitney, Trivinia Barber, Megan and Dan Fass, JJ Virgin, Jason Weisenthal, Michael Gottlieb, Joel Buckner, Jay Greenstein, Tony Ricciardi, Jay Gutnick, Tim Hawkins, Darryl Hicks, Jenny Shtipelman, Josh Katz, Alison Whitmire, Neal Lawson, Phil Williams, Katherine Liola, Erica Mechlinski, Tom Shieh, Tom Graham, Andrew Berkowitz, Emily Rasowsky, Diva Nagula, Jackie Bondanza, Andrew Berkowitz, Heather Wilde, Ken Williams, Ed Wotring, Megan Imbert, Nayia Pierrakos, Angie Fox, Kelly Gitter, Craig Villani, Dan Engle, Marissa Levin, Cara Foran, and Joel Bucker.

Mom, thank you for providing me with so much unconditional love growing up. Thank you for the opportunity and the space to shine and spread my wings, and to be whoever I wanted to be—even when you weren't sure about my choices. And thank you for taking such great care of Dad.

And to the rest of my nuclear family, Tricia and Dan Heck, and Jason and Meredith Coburn, thanks for your support and love over the years.

Bodie, thank you for keeping me company in the office during my many writing sessions. Your calm, peaceful energy always kept me grounded. I miss you a lot!

Melanie, you are my greatest muse, and creating a life where we get to spend as much quality time together as possible is my greatest inspiration. It has been so inspiring to watch and support you as you took on the NFL. Having a front-row seat to experience the most wonderful human on the planet is the greatest gift I have ever received.

I enjoy being a husband and a father more than anything else. Dexter and Caleb, you two are my greatest teachers, and my ability to spend more time with you is the number one benefit of creating a life of meaningful work. I feel like the luckiest guy in the world to be your father.

Notes

Introduction

1. Alliance for Lifetime Income, "Two-Third of Peak Baby Boomers Are Not Financially Prepared for Retirement," Protected Life Income, April 18, 2024, protectedincome.org/news/two-third-of-peak-baby-boomers-are-not-financially-prepared-for-retirement.
2. Alliance for Lifetime Income, "Two-Third of Peak Baby Boomers."
3. Alliance for Lifetime Income, "Two-Third of Peak Baby Boomers."
4. "New Research Finds 95 Percent of Millennials Not Saving Adequately for Retirement," National Institute on Retirement Security, press release, February 27, 2018, nirsonline.org/2018/02/new-research-finds-95-percent-of-millennials-not-saving-adequately-for-retirement.
5. Greenwald Research, *Generation X: Ready for Retirement?*, SOA Research Institute, February 2022, soa.org/globalassets/assets/files/resources/research-report/2022/2022-gen-x-retirement.pdf.
6. Juliana Menasce Horowitz and Kim Parker, "How Americans View Their Jobs," Pew Research Center, March 30, 2023, pewresearch.org/social-trends/2023/03/30/how-americans-view-their-jobs/.
7. *Vacation Deprivation Report 2023*, Expedia, 2023, expedia.com/stories/wp-content/uploads/2023/04/Expedia-Vacation-Deprivation-Global-Report-2023_Final-US-Small-compressed-1.pdf.
8. *Vacation Deprivation Report 2023*.

Chapter 1: Retirement Is Not Working

1. The assumptions used in this scenario are as follows.
   - Expected annual increase to income: 3 percent
   - Pre-retirement income desired in retirement: 70 percent (this amount is based on the household income earned during the year immediately before Tony's retirement)
   - Age at death: 95 (this translates to a 30-year retirement in the first scenario and 20 years in the second)
   - Rate of return on investments before retirement: 7 percent
   - Rate of return on investments during retirement: 6 percent
   - Rate of inflation: 3 percent
   - Assumptions are for a married person who plans to receive Social Security
2. Tim Urban, "The Tail End," *Wait but Why* (blog), December 11, 2015, waitbutwhy.com/2015/12/the-tail-end.html.
3. Esteban Ortiz-Ospina, Charlie Giattino, and Max Roser, "Time Use," Our World in Data, last updated February 2024, ourworldindata.org/time-use.

Chapter 2: How We Got Here

1. "Social Security History: Otto von Bismarck," US Social Security Administration, accessed February 29, 2024, ssa.gov/history/ottob.html.
2. Drake Baer, "Maybe You Should Just Never Retire," *The Cut*, June 6, 2016, thecut.com/2016/06/never-retire.html.
3. Gregory Wood, *Retiring Men: Manhood, Labor, and Growing Old in America, 1900–1960* (University Press of America, 2012).
4. Wood, *Retiring Men*.
5. Wood, *Retiring Men*.
6. Wood, *Retiring Men*.
7. Wood, *Retiring Men*.
8. Larry DeWitt, "Agency History: Research Note #17: The Townsend Plan's Pension Scheme," US Social Security Administration, December 2001, ssa.gov/history/townsendproblems.html.
9. Larry DeWitt, "Agency History: Research Note #3: Details of Ida May Fuller's Payroll Tax Contributions," US Social Security Administration, July 1996, ssa.gov/history/idapayroll.html.

10 DeWitt, "Agency History: Research Note #3."
11 "History of PBGC," Pension Benefit Guaranty Corporation, last updated November 16, 2023, pbgc.gov/about/who-we-are/pg/history-of-pbgc.
12 John C. Austin and Richard Kazis, "Rebuilding the Employment Security System for the Rust Belt That Created It," Brookings Institution, August 7, 2018, brookings.edu/articles/rebuilding-the-employment-security-system-for-the-rust-belt-that-created-it.
13 James A. Wooten, "'The Most Glorious Story of Failure in the Business': The Studebaker-Packard Corporation and the Origins of ERISA," *Buffalo Law Review* 49, no. 2 (April 2001): 683–739, doi.org/10.2139/ssrn.290812.
14 Lee Black, "ERISA: A Close Look at Misguided Legislation," *AMA Journal of Ethics* 10, no. 5 (May 1, 2008): 307–11, doi.org/10.1001/virtualmentor.2008.10.5.hlaw1-0805.
15 "The Economics Daily: Characteristics of Defined Benefit Retirement Plans in 2022," US Bureau of Labor Statistics, June 9, 2023, https://www.bls.gov/opub/ted/2023/characteristics-of-defined-benefit-retirement-plans-in-2022.htm.
16 Kathleen Elkins, "A Brief History of the 401(k), Which Changed How Americans Retire," CNBC, last updated January 5, 2017, cnbc.com/2017/01/04/a-brief-history-of-the-401k-which-changed-how-americans-retire.html.
17 Elkins, "A Brief History of the 401(k)."
18 "401(k) Resource Center," Investment Company Institute, accessed August 26, 2024, ici.org/401k.
19 Timothy W. Martin, "The Champions of the 401(k) Lament the Revolution They Started," *Wall Street Journal*, January 2, 2017, wsj.com/articles/the-champions-of-the-401-k-lament-the-revolution-they-started-1483382348.
20 Patty Kujawa, "A 'Father's' Wisdom: An Interview with Ted Benna," Workforce.com, January 20, 2012, workforce.com/news/a-fathers-wisdom-an-interview-with-ted-benna.
21 Elkins, "A Brief History of the 401(k)."
22 True Tamplin, "Understanding the Average 401(k) Balance by Age," Finance Strategists, last updated March 6, 2024, financestrategists.com/retirement-planning/401k/understanding-the-average-401k-balance-by-age.

23 John Elflein, "Life Expectancy for Men at the Age of 65 Years in the U.S. from 1960 to 2021," Statista, December 12, 2023, statista.com/statistics/266657/us-life-expectancy-for-men-aat-the-age-of-65-years-since-1960.
24 Ken Dychtwald, Robert Morison, and Katy Terveer, "Redesigning Retirement," *Harvard Business Review*, March–April 2024, hbr.org/2024/03/redesigning-retirement.
25 Dychtwald et al., "Redesigning Retirement."
26 Marc Schulz and Robert Waldinger, "An 85-Year Harvard Study on Happiness Found the No. 1 Retirement Challenge That 'No One Talks About,'" CNBC, March 10, 2024, cnbc.com/2023/03/10/85-year-harvard-happiness-study-found-the-biggest-downside-of-retirement-that-no-one-talks-about.html.
27 Jessica Stillman, "More and More People Are Unretiring—and Often, It Has Nothing to Do with Money," *Inc.*, October 9, 2023, inc.com/jessica-stillman/early-retirement-more-people-unretiring-often-nothing-to-do-with-money.html.
28 Stillman, "More and More People Are Unretiring."
29 Clare Ansberry, "Congrats on Your Retirement. Time to Find a New Job.," *Wall Street Journal*, February 17, 2024, wsj.com/health/wellness/retirement-costs-back-to-work-inflation-d84924f1.
30 Hillary Hoffower and Andy Kiersz, "Millennials Make More Money Than Any Other Generation Did at Their Age, but Are Way Less Wealthy. The Affordability Crisis Is to Blame.," *Business Insider*, September 22, 2021, businessinsider.com/millennials-highest-earning-generation-less-wealthy-boomers-2021-9.
31 Alicia H. Munnell and Wenliang Hou, "Will Millennials Be Ready for Retirement?" Center for Retirement Research at Boston College, January 23, 2018, crr.bc.edu/will-millennials-be-ready-for-retirement.

Chapter 3: Happiness versus Meaning

1 Wayne W. Dyer, *Your Erroneous Zones: Step-by-Step Advice for Escaping the Trap of Negative Thinking and Taking Control of Your Life* (William Morrow Paperbacks, 2001).
2 Mihaly Csikszentmihalyi, "Flow, the Secret to Happiness," filmed February 2004, TED video, 18:41, ted.com/talks/mihaly_csikszentmihalyi_flow_the_secret_to_happiness.

3. Mihaly Csikszentmihalyi, *Flow: The Psychology of Optimal Experience* (Harper & Row, 1990), 4.
4. Csikszentmihalyi, "Flow, the Secret to Happiness."
5. Roy F. Baumeister et al., "Some Key Differences between a Happy Life and a Meaningful Life," *Journal of Positive Psychology* 8, no. 6 (August 2013): 505–16, doi.org/10.1080/17439760.2013.830764.
6. Emily Esfahani Smith, "There's More to Life Than Being Happy," *The Atlantic*, January 9, 2013, theatlantic.com/health/archive/2013/01/theres-more-to-life-than-being-happy/266805.
7. Esfahani Smith, "There's More to Life."
8. Emily Esfahani Smith, "Meaning Is Healthier Than Happiness," *The Atlantic*, August 1, 2013, theatlantic.com/health/archive/2013/08/meaning-is-healthier-than-happiness/278250.
9. Esfahani Smith, "Meaning Is Healthier Than Happiness."
10. Esfahani Smith, "Meaning Is Healthier Than Happiness."
11. Esfahani Smith, "Meaning Is Healthier Than Happiness."
12. Andrea Atkins, "Peter Attia Offers Advice on How to Live a Long, Healthy Life," *Washington Post*, October 13, 2023, washingtonpost.com/wellness/2023/10/13/peter-attia-longevity-advice.
13. Ian Sample, "If They Could Turn Back Time: How Tech Billionaires Are Trying to Reverse the Ageing Process," *The Guardian*, February 17, 2022, theguardian.com/science/2022/feb/17/if-they-could-turn-back-time-how-tech-billionaires-are-trying-to-reverse-the-ageing-process.

Chapter 4: The Questions You Need to Be Asking

1. QY Research Medical, "Longevity and Anti-Senescence Therapy Market Size to Reach $44.2 BN by 2030," BioSpace, March 26, 2022, biospace.com/article/longevity-and-anti-senescence-therapy-market-size-to-reach-44-2-bn-by-2030.

Chapter 5: Your Many Options

1. Alex Hormozi, "In the Bible, before God gave Adam a wife, he gave him a job. We're made to work. For all of human history except for the last 75 years, we have worked until we die," X (formerly Twitter), February 21, 2024, x.com/AlexHormozi/status/1760391880280592731.

2. Ed Mylett, "You are more qualified to help people than you think you are. Read the quote AGAIN. It's not my quote, (I don't know [whose] it is originally). But it is one of the most profound things you'll ever read in your life," LinkedIn, September 14, 2022, linkedin.com/posts/edmylett_you-are-more-qualified-to-help-people-than-activity-6975823064785698817-NssF.
3. J.D. Roth, "How to Take a Sabbatical," *Get Rich Slowly*, last updated December 5, 2023, getrichslowly.org/how-to-take-a-mini-retirement-tips-and-tricks-from-timothy-ferriss.
4. Leo Almazora, "Nearly Half of Americans See a Slow Shift, Not a Clean Break in Retirement," InvestmentNews, May 7, 2024, investmentnews.com/retirement/news/nearly-half-of-americans-see-a-slow-shift-not-a-clean-break-in-retirement-253085.
5. Almazora, "Nearly Half of Americans."

Chapter 6: The Changing World of Work

1. Jan Hatzius et al., "The Potentially Large Effects of Artificial Intelligence on Economic Growth (Briggs/Kodnani)," Goldman Sachs' *Global Economics Analyst*, March 26, 2023, gspublishing.com/content/research/en/reports/2023/03/27/d64e052b-0f6e-45d7-967b-d7be35fabd16.html.
2. Kweilin Ellingrud et al., *Generative AI and the Future of Work in America*, McKinsey Global Institute, July 26, 2023, mckinsey.com/mgi/our-research/generative-ai-and-the-future-of-work-in-america.
3. James Manyika et al., "Jobs Lost, Jobs Gained: What the Future of Work Will Mean for Jobs, Skills, and Wages," McKinsey Global Institute, last updated July 16, 2024, mckinsey.com/featured-insights/future-of-work/jobs-lost-jobs-gained-what-the-future-of-work-will-mean-for-jobs-skills-and-wages. See also Ellingrud et al., *Generative AI and the Future of Work in America*.
4. "Upwork Study Finds 64 Million Americans Freelanced in 2023, Adding $1.27 Trillion to U.S. Economy," Upwork, news release, December 12, 2023, investors.upwork.com/news-releases/news-release-details/upwork-study-finds-64-million-americans-freelanced-2023-adding.
5. "Upwork Study Finds 64 Million Americans Freelanced."
6. "Half of Americans Prefer Opening a Small Business to Retirement, According to The UPS Store® Survey," The UPS Store, news release, May 6, 2019, theupsstore.com/about/pressroom/inside-small-business-survey.

7   "Half of Americans Prefer Opening a Small Business."
8   Tom Agan, "Why Innovators Get Better with Age," *New York Times*, March 30, 2013, nytimes.com/2013/03/31/jobs/why-innovators-get-better-with-age.html.
9   Victoria Masterson, "Future of Jobs 2023: These Are the Most In-Demand Skills Now—and Beyond," World Economic Forum, May 1, 2023, weforum.org/agenda/2023/05/future-of-jobs-2023-skills.
10 "Hybrid Work," Gallup, accessed October 11, 2024, gallup.com/401384/indicator-hybrid-work.aspx.

Chapter 8: Insurance

1   Allan Checkoway, "Chance of Becoming Disabled," chap. 1 in *A Lawyer's Guide to Filing Long-Term Disability Claims and Appeals* (American Bar Association, 2019).
2   Checkoway, "Chance of Becoming Disabled."
3   Checkoway, "Chance of Becoming Disabled."
4   Kim Painter, "Understanding Long-Term Care Insurance," AARP, last updated February 6, 2024, aarp.org/caregiving/financial-legal/info-2021/understanding-long-term-care-insurance.html.
5   Aliza Vigderman and Makenna Cook, "Uninsured Motorists Statistics: 2022 U.S. Report," AutoInsurance.com, last updated July 24, 2024, autoinsurance.com/research/uninsured-motorists.
6   Kayda Norman, "State Minimum Car Insurance Requirements," NerdWallet, last updated February 5, 2024, nerdwallet.com/article/insurance/minimum-car-insurance-requirements.

Chapter 9: Investment Strategies

1   "Americans Believe They Will Need $1.46 Million to Retire Comfortably According to Northwestern Mutual 2024 Planning & Progress Study," Northwestern Mutual, news release, April 2, 2024, news.northwesternmutual.com/2024-04-02-Americans-Believe-They-Will-Need-1-46-Million-to-Retire-Comfortably-According-to-Northwestern-Mutual-2024-Planning-Progress-Study.
2   "Time, Not Timing, Is What Matters," Capital Group, accessed June 5, 2024, capitalgroup.com/individual/planning/investing-fundamentals/time-not-timing-is-what-matters.html.

Chapter 10: Investing in You

1. Susan L. Worley, "The Extraordinary Importance of Sleep," *Pharmacy and Therapeutics* 43, no. 12 (December 2018): 758–63, ncbi.nlm.nih.gov/pmc/articles/PMC6281147.
2. Lawrence Epstein and Alice Cai, "Shorter Dream-Stage Sleep May Be Related to Earlier Death," *Harvard Health* (blog), September 18, 2020, health.harvard.edu/blog/shorter-dream-stage-sleep-may-be-related-to-earlier-death-2020091820932.
3. Peter Attia, "#217: Exercise, VO2 Max, and Longevity | Mike Joyner, M.D.," *The Peter Attia Drive* (podcast), August 8, 2022, 1:52:45, peterattiamd.com/mikejoyner.
4. Attia, "#217: Exercise, VO2 Max, and Longevity."
5. Jeff Grabmeier, "Think Leisure Is a Waste? That May Not Bode Well for Your Mental Health," *Ohio State News*, news release, August 23, 2021, news.osu.edu/think-leisure-is-a-waste-that-may-not-bode-well-for-your-mental-health.
6. Michael Rucker, "Why You Need More Fun in Your Life, According to Science," *Michael Rucker Ph.D.* (blog), December 11, 2016, michaelrucker.com/having-fun/why-you-need-more-fun-in-your-life.
7. Julie Scharper, "Lighten Up—According to Science, It's Good for You," *Johns Hopkins Magazine*, Summer 2016, hub.jhu.edu/magazine/2016/summer/neuroscience-of-fun.
8. Scharper, "Lighten Up."
9. Lindsay Kohler, "Finally, Proof That Happiness Does Make Us Work Better," *Forbes*, November 28, 2023, forbes.com/sites/lindsaykohler/2023/11/28/finally-proof-that-happiness-does-make-us-work-better.
10. Lewis Howes, "Harnessing the Power of Stress & Anxiety | Dr. Wendy Suzuki," *The School of Greatness* (podcast), September 23, 2023, 1:41:24, podcastdisclosed.com/harnessing-the-power-of-stress-anxiety-dr-wendy-suzuki-lewis-howes-the-school-of-greatness.
11. Alexa Mikhail, "Neuroscientist Andrew Huberman Says These 5 Daily Habits Are Key to Optimal Mental and Physical Health," *Fortune*, September 5, 2023, fortune.com/well/2023/09/05/andrew-huberman-daily-habits-optimal-mental-physical-health.
12. Nina Avramova, "Friends and Family May Help Italians Live Healthier and Longer," CNN, last updated May 9, 2019, cnn.com/2019/05/09/health/social-connections-health-benefits-intl/index.html.

13 Avramova, "Friends and Family May Help."
14 Nicole K. Valtorta et al., "Loneliness and Social Isolation as Risk Factors for Coronary Heart Disease and Stroke: Systematic Review and Meta-Analysis of Longitudinal Observational Studies," *Heart* 102, no. 13 (April 18, 2016): 1009–16, doi.org/10.1136/heartjnl-2015-308790.
15 Tzvi Doron, "Friends and Longevity: The Science of Social Connection," Ro, last updated April 8, 2020, https://ro.co/health-guide/friends-and-longevity.
16 Hajdi Moche and Daniel Västfjäll, "To Give or to Take Money? The Effects of Choice on Prosocial Spending and Happiness," *Journal of Positive Psychology* 17, no. 5 (2022): 742–53, doi.org/10.1080/17439760.2021.1940248. See also Lara B. Aknin et al., "Does Spending Money on Others Promote Happiness? A Registered Replication Report," *Journal of Personality and Social Psychology* 119, no. 2 (August 2020): e15–e26, doi.org/10.1037/pspa0000191.

Index

Airbnb, 110
Alliance for Lifetime Income, 5–6
Allianz Life, 100
American Express, 40
Attia, Peter, 56, 184

Baby Boomers, 45, 100
Baer, Jay, 82–84
Batterson, Mark, 27
Benna, Ted, 42
Bismarck, Otto von, 35–36, 63
Buckley, Jim, 111
Bureau of Labor Statistics, 41

CADRE, 86–87
Clark, Faryn, 79–81
Coburn, Derek, 26, 85–86, 95, 134, 195
Coburn, Melanie, 85, 86, 95, 134, 195
Conley, Chip, 110
Cope, Stephen, 100
COVID-19 pandemic, 82, 96, 111–14
Csikszentmihalyi, Mihaly, 50–51

Daily Dad (Holiday), 30
debt, 6, 45, 123–24

dementia, 1–3, 72, 128, 149–50
Department of Health and Human Services, 146
Dyer, Wayne, 50

80-20 Rule, 86
Employee Retirement Income Security Act (ERISA), 41
Expedia *Vacation Deprivation Report*, 7

Ferriss, Tim, 91
Financial Independence, Retire Early (FIRE) movement, 45
financial planning: conversations with partner, 130–33; debt management, 122–24; emergency savings, 121–22; estate planning, 133–35; focus on present, 120–21; insurance and investment strategy, 127; mortgage management, 124–26; need for, 119–20, 204; parental care, 128–30; trustee, selection of, 135–36. *See also* insurance; investment strategies
The 4-Hour Workweek (Ferriss), 91
Fuller, Ida May, 38

Future of Jobs Report (World Economic Forum), 108

Gen Xers, 6, 45, 100
Gen Zers, 46
Gilbert, Daniel, 61
Give and Take (Grant), 52
Goldman Sachs, 105
Gottlieb, Michael, 96–98
Graham, Tom, 87–88
Grant, Adam, 52, 114
The Great Work of Your Life (Cope), 100

happiness vs. meaning: flow states, 50–51; happiness, pursuit of, 50; health effects, 52–55; longevity, 55–56; meaningful life, 52, 59–60; taking vs. giving, 52
Holiday, Ryan, 30
Hormozi, Alex, 77–78
Huberman, Andrew, 195–96

Inside Small Business Survey (UPS Store), 106–108
insurance: disability, 144–45; health, 150–51; liability, 151–52; life, 138–39; life, term, 139–41; life, whole, 141–42; long-term care, 146–50; need for, 137, 153
investment strategies: annuities, 159–61; compounding interest, 171–74; need for, 155–56; planning options, 156–57, 176; required minimum distributions (RMDs), 161–62; return on investment, 174–75; risk, 168–71; Roth IRA, 157–58, 167–68; tax buckets, 164–68

Joyner, Michael, 184

Lord, Janet, 56

Maté, Gabor, 197
McKernan, Philip, 78
McKinsey Global Institute, 105
Millennials, 6, 45–46, 100, 109
Modern Elder Academy, 110
Mylett, Ed, 89
The Myth of Normal (Maté), 197

National Institute on Retirement Security, 6
Networking Is Not Working (Coburn), 26, 85

Originals (Grant), 114

PayPal, 168
Pew Research Center, 7

retirement: ageism, 36–37; creation of concept, 35–38; Employee Retirement Income Security Act (ERISA), 41; life expectancy, 43, 47; private pensions, 40–41; psychological effects of, 71–72; Revenue Act of 1978, 41–42; Social Security Act, 38–40, 68–69; Townsend Plan, 37–38; traditional retirement, myth of, 8–10, 14, 57–59, 201; unretiring, 43–45. *See also* retirement alternatives; retirement planning; work-life balance
retirement alternatives: career transitioning, 78–81; consulting/coaching, 87–89; 80-20 rule, 86; fulfillment, pursuit of, 78, 81, 102–103; life's calling, pursuit of, 95–98; mini-retirements, 91–95; pivoting, 100–101; sabbaticals, 89–90; side businesses, 81–87; slowing down, 98–100
Retirement Income Institute, 5–6

retirement planning: family milestones, 73; financial calculator, 73–75; financial industry assumptions, 61–62; 401(k) plans, 42–43, 127, 156–58; health, changes in, 72; individual retirement account (IRA), 157, 158, 162, 167; inflation, 69; lifestyle, 64; longevity, 69–71; opportunity costs, 25–26; required income, 66–68; saving, 5–7, 11, 20, 22–25; saving, demographic variations in, 6, 45–46; triggering events, 11–13. *See also* financial planning
Revenue Act of 1978, 41–42
Roosevelt, Franklin D., 38
Ruhlin, John, 199
Rule of 72, 173–74

Social Security Act, 38–40, 68–69
Stibitz, Sara, 13
student debt, 6, 45
Stumbling on Happiness (Gilbert), 61
Suzuki, Wendy, 195

Thiel, Peter, 168
Townsend, Francis, 37–38

United States (US): Bureau of Labor Statistics, 41; Department of Health and Human Services, 146; Employee Retirement Income Security Act (ERISA), 41; Revenue Act of 1978, 41–42; Social Security Act, 38–40, 68–69
UPS Store Inside Small Business Survey, 106–108
Upwork, 106
Urban, Tim, 26

Vacation Deprivation Report (Expedia), 7

Vanguard, 43
Vaynerchuk, Gary, 82

Wait but Why (Urban), 26
Williams, Ati, 92–93
Wisdom @ Work (Conley), 110
work: AI and automation, 105–106; as change agency, 114–15; COVID-19, influence on, 111–14; entrepreneurship, 106–107; freelancing, 106, 109; human skills, 108; skills and training, 109–111
work-life balance: exercise, 184–85; friendship and connection, 195–98; having fun, 185–90; lifelong learning, 191; opportunity costs, 2–3, 26–27, 29–31, 34, 178; philanthropy, 198–99; primary relationship, 193–95; quality of life, 6–7, 11, 32–34, 46, 201–202, 204; self-care, 179–82; sleep, 182–84. *See also* happiness vs. meaning; work
World Economic Forum, 108

LET'S STAY CONNECTED

This is a collaborative effort—let's retire retirement together!

Learn with me
Find more ideas and the latest research on how we can all live our lives to the fullest—now and later—at **derekcoburn.com**.

Reach out
If you have questions or success stories to share, please email me at **derek@derekcoburn.com**.

Spread the word
If you are moved to share anything you found helpful in this book, please use the hashtag **#neverretire** to join the conversation.

About the Authors

DEREK COBURN is a financial advisor with over twenty-five years of experience. His passion for connecting remarkable professionals led him, along with his wife, Melanie, to start a professional community for CEOs and entrepreneurs called CADRE. He enjoys traveling and live music, and cherishes being a husband and father above all else. Coburn is the bestselling author of *Networking Is Not Working*. He lives in Virginia with Melanie and their two sons.

SARA STIBITZ is a *New York Times*-bestselling collaborative writer and creative coach. Many of her books have won awards from Nautilus, Bloomsbury, Axiom, Reviewers' Choice, Indie Excellence, and Independent Press. She has a keen ability to draw out meaningful stories from her clients and brings a blend of empathy and intuition to every project. To learn more about her work, go to sarastibitz.com.